Del Pueblo

NUMBER TWENTY-ONE: GULF COAST BOOKS

SPONSORED BY TEXAS A&M UNIVERSITY-CORPUS CHRISTI

JOHN W. TUNNELL JR., GENERAL EDITOR

A list of titles in this series appears at the back of the book.

Del Pueblo

A History of Houston's Hispanic Community

THOMAS H. KRENECK

Texas A&M University Press

COLLEGE STATION

LIBRARY OF CONGRESS CATALOGING-IN-PUBLICATION DATA

Kreneck, Thomas H.
  Del Pueblo : a history of Houston's Hispanic community / Thomas H. Kreneck. —
Texas A&M University Press ed.
        p. cm. — (Gulf Coast books ; no. 21)
  "New, revised edition."—Summary, CIP data view.
  Original edition published by Houston International University, 1989.
  Includes bibliographical references and index.
  ISBN-13: 978-1-60344-692-1 (cloth : alk. paper)
  ISBN-10: 1-60344-692-3 (cloth : alk. paper)
  ISBN-13: 978-1-60344-735-5 (e-book)
  ISBN-10: 1-60344-735-0 (e-book)
  1. Hispanic Americans—Texas—Houston—History—Pictorial works.
2. Hispanic Americans—Texas—Houston—History.   3. Houston (Tex.)—
History—Pictorial works.   4. Houston (Tex.)—History.   5. Houston (Tex.)—
Pictorial works.   I. Title.   II. Series: Gulf Coast books ; no. 21.
  F394.H89K57 2012
  305.8968'07307641411—dc23
  2011047422

Frontispiece: Members of the singing and theatrical group of Magnolia Park, ca. 1928.
Courtesy Houston Metropolitan Reserach Center, Houston Public Library, Chairez
Family Collection.

To those people of
Houston's Hispanic community who,
during the 1970s and 1980s,
shared their memories and historical materials with me
and contributed to this book.

Contents

Preface to the
Texas A&M University Press Edition

THE PUBLICATION OF *Del Pueblo: A History of Houston's Hispanic Community* by Texas A&M University Press is a revised and updated second edition of the book that appeared in 1989. The initial volume carried the title *Del Pueblo: A Pictorial History of Houston's Hispanic Community* because it included more than 240 images. This second edition contains fewer illustrations in proportion to the text, thus making it more balanced in its presentation and requiring the abbreviated title. While the 1989 edition concluded at that date, the present survey ends at the year 2000.

The 1989 volume and this second edition resulted in large measure from work I did in the late 1970s and 1980s, when I served as an archivist and then First Assistant of the Houston Metropolitan Research Center (HMRC) of the Houston Public Library. In 1978, I founded and until December 1990 developed HMRC's Mexican American archival component. During those twelve years I had the privilege of documenting the history of Houston's Hispanic community as I solicited the donation of many archival and manuscript collections, historic photographs, oral history recordings, print materials, and other items from that population. The associations that I made with people and the activities involved in the effort formed one of the most meaningful professional experiences of my career. *Del Pueblo* therefore represents my tribute to HMRC and to the community whose history this book attempts to portray.

I made the initial edition of *Del Pueblo* a pictorial history because my collecting efforts had yielded an abundance of old photographs. The many family collections proved especially fruitful in the number of images they contained. Coming directly from the residents, such photos portrayed Hispanics as they saw themselves rather than as outsiders would have viewed them. This dimension, it seemed to me, made the photographs more worthy as a method of understanding a community. My own special interest in photos as documentation added to this focus. The resulting positive acceptance of the book by the people who had donated materials to the Mexican American archival component validated my belief. The public unveiling of *Del Pueblo* in 1989, held in the large reception area on the top floor of Houston's *El Mercado Del Sol,* attracted more than eight hundred people. This turnout proved most gratifying to all of us involved in the publication.

As indicated by the credit lines, I supplemented the historic images in the book with photographs I personally took of the community during the 1980s. Indulging my own interest in taking photographs endeared the book to me even more.

For a combination of reasons, I chose to publish the first edition of *Del Pueblo* through Houston International University (HIU), a community-based institution initially founded on the university-without-walls concept. Those motives included my involvement with the solidarity movement in support of the people of Central America and my impatience with traditional academia. Also, I felt that HIU, under then-president Leonel J. Castillo, represented a more grassroots approach. The other many folks who contributed to that initial effort will be thanked in the original Preface that follows.

The 1989 edition of *Del Pueblo* has been out of print for many years, and numerous individuals have requested that it be reissued in some form. As mentioned above, the second edition contains fewer photographs, but I have retained what I term the essential images from the first book. To help make it a more updated version, the second edition also contains some images from the 1990s and from earlier decades that the first version did not. I hope that the second edition will meet the expectations of those kind folks who wanted to see it released once again. The photographs remain a key element in this volume for conveying the community's history.

I wish to thank a number of people for assisting with the publication of the second edition, including Cecilia G. Venable for her expertise in reproducing the images; Dr. Arnoldo De León, my constant comrade, for his thorough editing of the manuscript; Dr. Chrystel K. Pit, Dr. Guadalupe San Miguel Jr., and Dr. Roberto Treviño for new historical insights; Dr. David J. Webb, genealogist extraordinaire, for his sleuthing pertinent records; Dr. Gayle Davies for crucial research assistance; Douglas Weiskopf for his recollections; Steve Gonzales of the *Houston Chronicle* for arranging the permission to use important images; Dr. C. Elaine Cummins and my brother James R. Kreneck for their continual encouragement; as well as Benny Martínez, Loretta Martínez Williams, Linda A. Sáenz, and my many other friends in the Houston Hispanic history circles for their support. I also want to thank Dr. John W. Tunnell Jr., General Editor of the Texas A&M University–Corpus Christi Gulf Coast Series, for his sponsorship.

Finally, and equally important, I want to express my special gratitude to the Houston Metropolitan Research Center, its able former chief administrator Kemo Curry, its current acting manager Elizabeth Sargent, and its staff, including Amber Seely and Joel Draut, for supporting this second edition. I am deeply grateful for their help and for Ms. Curry's (and later Ms. Sargent's) permission to use the images included in this present volume. HMRC remains a treasure house of Houston's history, and it will always hold a profound meaning to me. I am grateful to have been part of its early development, and I am extremely proud of its current work under Ms. Curry, Ms. Sargent, their staff, and its many supporters.

THOMAS H. KRENECK
Corpus Christi, 2011

Preface to the Original Edition

THE HISTORY OF THE HISPANIC COMMUNITY in Houston, Texas, is an interesting and important chapter in the story of Hispanics in the United States. It provides a major example of the urbanization of one of the most vital ethnic groups in our modern nation. It likewise represents a process of what might readily be called the Hispanization of the Bayou City because so many Latinos came to reside there.

Fortunately several noted historians (chiefly professors Arnoldo De León and F. Arturo Rosales) have provided us with scholarly analyses of the topic. Their work, in combination with that of sociologists, anthropologists, political scientists, and other academicians, has enlarged our grasp of this ethnic urban community. As time progresses, other scholars will no doubt contribute to this expanding body of literature.

I wrote *Del Pueblo* as a public history—a volume that will make an understanding of Houston's Hispanic heritage accessible to the average reader as well as to the academic audience. As such, it emphasizes individuals and their roles in their community's development. Because I believe in the adage that one picture is worth a thousand words, *Del Pueblo* combines photographs, other visuals, and written text. Seeing the images of the people in their urban surroundings makes their stories more vivid, more personal, and more human, and one can more readily comprehend the evolution of a fluid, sophisticated, complex community and how it has become an integral part of a dynamic city. It is my hope that this volume conveys a sense of the especially long road Houstonians of Mexican descent have traveled to improve their condition and provide the basis for all Hispanic people who call Houston their home.

Many people have directly contributed to my knowledge of Houston's Hispanic past. I would like to note the special insight given by my academic colleagues, particularly historians Arnoldo De León, F. Arturo Rosales, Roberto Treviño, Marilyn D. Rhinehart, Manuel Urbina II, and Margaret Henson; sociologists Tatcho Mindiola Jr. and Nestor Rodríguez; psychologist Marie Theresa Hernández; educators Luis R. Cano and Lorenzo Cano; publisher Nicolás Kanellos; litterateurs Sylvia Pena and Julián Olivares; and anthropologist Margarita Melville. I especially want to thank professors Rosales and De León for helping me frame my ideas for Chapters 4 and 8, respectively. I also want to express my gratitude to Louis J. Marchiafava for his valuable help, encouragement, and advice; Don E. Carleton and Joan T. Dusard for their intellectual comradeship; and Noble Enete and Deborah A. Bauer for their special insights. The many undergraduate students in the Chicano History courses that I taught during the 1980s for Dr. Tatcho Mindiola at the Mexican American Studies Program at the University of Houston also provided me with inspiration and require my appreciation.

Photographers Carlos Antonio Rios and the late Luciaan Blyaert, past librarian of the *Houston Chronicle* Sherry Adams, and former librarian of the *Houston Post* Kathy Foley, deserve special mention for their contributions.

My two original manuscript editors, Nancy Hadley and Dian Redford, made it a much more readable book. They ensured that the prose properly conveyed content. Nancy's editorial patience helped me in untold ways.

So many other people have informed my understanding of this topic that I have listed their names in the Appendix, in appreciation of their valuable assistance. As participants in Houston's Hispanic history, they have shared their insights and experiences with me, helped locate and identify many of the visuals, and ensured the public-history nature of the finished product. I apologize if anyone who contributed has been omitted. As mentioned in the Introduction of this second edition, many of the photographs are selected from the Mexican American archival component of the Houston Metropolitan Research Center (HMRC) of the Houston Public Library. It bears repeating that these items were generously donated by people whose aim it was that Houston's Hispanic tradition be fully documented and appreciated by present and future generations. Unless indicated otherwise, all collections cited in the captions are on deposit at the HMRC. I hope that my incorporation of select visuals accurately portrays that rich history and thus expands public awareness of that important part of our heritage.

The sponsorship of Southwestern Bell Foundation and Houston International University made possible the first edition of *Del Pueblo* in

1989. Southwestern Bell Foundation, through Gloria Delgado, then Area Manager of External Affairs, Southwestern Bell Telephone Company, generously provided the major funding for its publication. Houston International University, through the efforts of its then-president Leonel J. Castillo, served as publisher. Both of these individuals that year provided crucial support for the project and were largely responsible for its successful production. I will always be grateful to them both.

Finally, any errors of fact or interpretation are mine alone.

Del Pueblo

Introduction

UNTIL THE LATE TWENTIETH CENTURY, Hispanic tradition and culture were not readily associated in the popular imagination with Houston, Texas. The Spanish Mexican influence in the urban United States seemed most pronounced in such places as Los Angeles, Tucson, Albuquerque, and San Antonio. These towns ranked among the many population centers in the present American Southwest that Hispanic colonists had settled when that region formed part of the Spanish Empire and the Republic of Mexico, long before Houston came into being.

Despite its more recent origins, Houston today hosts a large Hispanic presence with a rich, varied history. Houston's Hispanic community is a twentieth-century phenomenon with nineteenth-century precursors. Its history is essentially that of Mexican Americans because they have formed the overwhelming majority of the Bayou City's Spanish-speaking residents.

Founded as a frontier town by John and Augustus Chapman Allen in late 1836 after the war for Texas independence, Houston developed throughout that century largely devoid of Hispanic influence. Far from the centers of Spanish Mexican population to the southwest, early Houston was a town marked by a combination of Old South culture and the nineteenth-century ethic of American westward expansion. During the 1880s, however, people of Mexican heritage moved to Houston in significant numbers, establishing an urban presence of fewer than five hundred people by 1900. These early settlers ensured that Hispanics would thereafter be part of the Houston scene. In turn, they encountered a particular brand of Anglo-American, anti-Mexican prejudice that had been firmly established during the 1800s and would present obstacles to Mexican American advancement in Houston society. On the other hand, they benefitted from a level of acceptance offered by a port city whose societal fluidity granted opportunity to all comers. In short, these Hispanics formed enduring associations with one another and many of their non-Latino neighbors.

Much like the rest of Houston, the Hispanic community came into its own during the first part of the new century. After 1900, rapid growth and change were the order of the day for Houston in general and for its Mexican population in particular. Houston's Mexican Americans, as a group, remained in constant flux, reflecting a changing urban environment.

Immigration from the Mexican Revolution of 1910 and simultaneous economic developments in Houston caused the population of Mexicans in the Bayou City to grow and evolve into viable *barrios* by the 1920s, the seedtime of Mexican American urbanization. In that decade, Houston's *la colonia Mexicana* (or *el pueblo Mexicano,* as it was alternately called in those years) permanently marked the city's cultural and demographic landscape. The Great Depression of the 1930s temporarily slowed this growth, but it was never halted. Indeed, Mexican Houstonians during the 1930s clearly identified with their city even as they struggled against the hard times and discrimination they so often confronted. Their participation in the American effort in World War II even more firmly linked their destinies with the United States.

Accelerated growth during and after the Second World War expanded the numbers and influence of Houston's Latin Americans (as they were then commonly called). By the 1950s, they had articulate, highly visible civic and business leaders who called attention to their community's many difficulties. In turn, many Anglo friends and associates supported and advanced these efforts toward improvement of conditions for Hispanics.

The years from the 1930s through the 1950s witnessed the development of a vibrant, bicultural Mexican American society in Houston—one that retained portions of its Mexican heritage and Spanish language yet adopted many of the traits of Anglo-Houston. The increased involvement by Mexican Houstonians in mainstream society was spearheaded by their expanding middle class and was best exemplified by the civic efforts of such organizations as the League of United Latin American Citizens (LULAC).

The postwar aspirations of Houston's Mexican Americans took definite shape in the 1960s and early 1970s during a time of unprecedented political and social activism. This period of protest, symbolized by the use of the term "Chicano" as a more militant form of self-designation, involved many strident grassroots organizations and produced citywide Mexican American political leadership for the first time. Mexican Americans translated their increasing numbers into representation as precinct judges, on the Houston School Board of Trustees, as Harris County constables, as judges on various levels of the court systems, as state legislators, and in other elected and appointed positions.

By the mid-1980s, the Spanish-speaking population of the Houston metropolitan region had reached an estimated one-half million. This large number included thousands of relative newcomers to the city not only from other parts of the United States and Mexico but also from the Caribbean and South and Central America. While Mexican Americans continued to comprise the majority of the Hispanic community, people from El Salvador, Honduras, Guatemala, Cuba, Puerto Rico, Columbia, and other Latin American nations considerably augmented this population. They added to the Hispanic flavor of the nation's fourth largest city. They gave additional meaning to the term "Decade of the Hispanic," a phrase used at that time to connote the anticipated clout of the entire ethnic group.

As of the year 2000, Houston's Hispanic community continued to grow and develop. Individuals who had played leadership positions gave way to a new generation of Latinos assuming positions of authority. Assimilation and acculturation remained a constant feature. Yet suburban neighborhoods far from the inner city have taken on a decided Latino ambience brought about by upwardly mobile Spanish-speaking homeowners and apartment dwellers. Just as the rest of Houston, the Hispanic community has a future that cannot truly be predicted.

From fewer than five hundred in 1900, Houston's Hispanic population by 2000 had grown to more than seven hundred thirty thousand. Hispanics have maintained a significant presence in Houston for more than a century, and they have evolved into a diverse modern community. Their influence and contributions, already great, will undoubtedly increase in the years to come as the city witnesses its Hispanization, a phenomenon that would have seemed unimaginable when the Allen brothers established Houston on the banks of Buffalo Bayou many years before.

The following chapters, through a mixture of text and illustrations, will convey a sense of Houston's Hispanic history as I perceive it. The events, places, and people depicted in this book should, by illuminating past development, provide a better understanding of our present circumstances and thus, in some small way, help to brighten the road to the future.

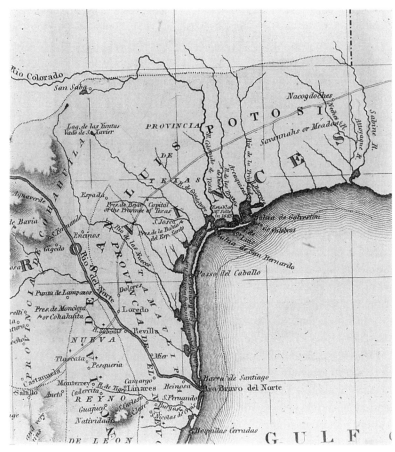

La Provincia de Tejas (Texas), after three hundred years of Spanish rule, showed its Hispanic imprint in the names of rivers, towns, and other geographic locations. The *presidio*-mission complex called *El Orcoquisac* (spelled "Arcaquisas" on this 1827 map) on the Trinity River was the only Spanish settlement in the Harris County vicinity.

CHAPTER ONE

A Peripheral Spanish Imprint

ALTHOUGH TEXAS WAS A POSSESSION of Spain for three hundred years, the Spanish never founded lasting settlements in the immediate Houston area. Established after Spain lost its North American empire, Houston would not initially have the Hispanic traditions that marked Laredo, Nacogdoches, La Bahía (Goliad), San Antonio, and El Paso. Nonetheless, to guard East Texas against French incursion from Louisiana, the Spanish charted the region during the early 1700s, founded a short-lived presidio-mission complex approximately thirty-five miles east of modern Houston, and left their imprint by naming major rivers and other local geographic features.

After the Spanish claimed the Texas coast in 1519, their interest in East Texas lay dormant until the French threatened the region during the late 1600s. In the ensuing contest for empire, Spain dispatched expeditions as far as Louisiana to maintain its hold on the territory. One such effort against French traders led to the formal establishment of *Presidio San Agustin de Ahumada* on May 26, 1756, on the east bank of the Trinity River near its mouth. After months of delay, the Spaniards constructed Mission *Nuestra Señora de la Luz del Orcoquisac* not far from the garrison. Built to minister to the local Orcoquiza Indians, this mission was a simple log chapel with a four-arched porch coated with plaster.

The *presidio*-mission site with its thirty soldiers and two Franciscan friars came to be known as *El Orcoquisac*. Located in Chambers County near Wallisville, it was the only Spanish settlement in the modern-day Harris County vicinity. As at the other missions of East Texas, the Spanish suffered illnesses and deaths at *El Orcoquisac* from the unhealthy climate, insect bites, and polluted water supply. Such inhospitable circumstances contributed to the lack of any lasting Spanish influence in this northern reach of *Nueva España*. In 1766, a hurricane destroyed the mission and *presidio*, both of which Spanish authorities soon restored at great expense and difficulty.

Spain's New World possessions, stretching from *Tierra del Fuego* to Kansas, proved too extensive, its resources too limited, and the region's attractions too few to warrant permanent occupation of the Harris County area. A civilian settlement of fifty families from the Saltillo region proposed for *Santa Rosa de Alcazán,* at the point where Santa Rosa Spring flowed into the San Jacinto River, never materialized.

The Orcoquiza and other Indians were either apathetic or hostile to Spanish efforts to Christianize them. In addition, control over the Louisiana Territory passed to Spain after 1763 and, thus, the French no longer posed a threat.

Accordingly, both *Presidio Ahumada* and Mission *El Orcoquisac* were abandoned by 1772. The *padres* and soldiers pulled back to San Antonio, leaving behind wooden remains of the chapel, fort, and other buildings, which Gulf Coast storms soon swept away. Dense East Texas foliage rapidly overgrew the *presidio*-mission cemetery and plowed ground where the Spaniards had their reluctant Indian charges raise corn.

Although Spanish authorities sent soldiers to reoccupy the location after 1803, by the twentieth century *El Orcoquisac* and *Presidio Ahumada* were no more than archeological sites, emblematic of the lack of permanent influence the Spanish Empire had in the Houston area. In the 1990s, those who wanted to see the location where *El Orcoquisac* once stood faced a lengthy, difficult hike.

Spanish place names dating from that colonial period represent a more lasting imprint on the greater Houston vicinity. One can hardly enter the metropolitan region without crossing a river whose name is a perpetual reminder of the first European owners of the area. To the southwest is the Brazos River (*Río de los Brazos de Dios*), while to the north and east is the San Jacinto (*Río San Jacinto*). Both streams, like so many others in *Tejas,* were discovered, named, and explored by Spanish expeditions. The San Jacinto River supposedly received its name because explorers first saw it on the holy day of Saint Hyacinth. The *Brazos de Dios* (Arms of God) was so named when its fresh waters saved its discoverers from dying of thirst.

Southwest of Houston, Spanish explorers charted and named Galveston Bay (*Bahía de Galveston*) in 1785 in honor of Bernardo de Gálvez, the royal governor of New Orleans. The name was applied to the island, town, and county that are Houston's important neighbors. Also, probably the oldest place name in Harris County, Atascosito Crossing, on the San Jacinto River, formed part of the *Atascosito* Road, established by the Spaniards in 1757 as their military highway to East Texas.

Because of the peripheral nature of Spanish influence, people often fail to remember that Spain owned and explored the Harris County region even though it did not play a direct role in the development of the Houston Hispanic community as it did in other parts of Texas.

Captain Juan Seguin led the only company composed mainly of native-born Texas rebels under Sam Houston at the Battle of San Jacinto. Photo courtesy of Texas State Library, Austin.

CHAPTER TWO

In the Shadow of San Jacinto

BETWEEN THE YEAR MEXICO gained its independence in 1821 and the establishment of Houston in late 1836, Anglo-American settlers from the United States came to out-populate Texas Hispanics. The Battle of San Jacinto, which ended the Texas Revolution in 1836, took place only a few miles from the future site of Houston, emblematic of how securely the province was in the hands of the newcomers. Houston was founded shortly after the Battle of San Jacinto and during the mid-1800s was largely devoid of Hispanic influence; however, its few Mexican residents saw the development of anti-Mexican sentiment that became the basis for prejudice against future generations of Hispanic Houstonians.

With Mexican independence in 1821, ownership of the Harris County region passed from Spain to Mexico. But Mexico's tenuous political condition, its limited resources, and the distance between Mexico City and East Texas continued to stymie Hispanic influence there. The French challenge to the region had been replaced after 1803 by a more serious threat from the expanding United States. The fledgling Mexican nation tried to buttress already established frontier settlements in Texas, positioned new military garrisons where it could, and simultaneously tried to introduce fresh settlers. The Harris County area became part of the Mexican state of *Coahuila-Tejas* in 1824 and received its first permanent settlement under the auspices of Mexico. These early residents were not, however, native Mexicans.

Developing a plan that had germinated with Spanish officials during the final days of the empire, Mexican authorities by 1822 allowed Anglo-American newcomers into Texas as a buffer against U.S. expansion. Although this plan would later result in detriment to Mexico, these initial settlers were loyal citizens to their adopted Mexico and relations between the Anglos and Mexican officials seemed relatively tranquil. As part of the colony of the *empresario* Stephen F. Austin, by 1822 between fifteen and twenty Anglo-American families made their homes along the San Jacinto River and Buffalo Bayou in present-day Harris County. Some thirty-two more people received grants from the Mexican government in 1824 on Cedar and Buffalo Bayous and the San Jacinto River. After 1833, under Mexican rule, this general area came to be the District of Harrisburg, so named for the first town laid out in the region.

Harrisburg was established at the confluence of Buffalo and Braes Bayous around 1826, followed after 1830 by Lynchburg, Stafford's Prairie House, and New Kentucky. This area came solidly under Anglo influence by the early 1830s when conflict developed between Mexican officials and the Texas colonists. Native Mexican presence, ascendant further to the southwest in the San Antonio region, was nonexistent in the Harrisburg District. So rapidly had Anglo-American settlers entered *Tejas* during the Mexican period that by 1836 they outnumbered native Mexicans ten to one. The Texas War for Independence, concluded at the Battle of San Jacinto near present-day Houston on April 21, 1836, culminated in the domination of Texas by Anglo-Americans—a process that had begun in 1822.

By the time of the Texas Revolution, Anglo settlers not only had established their position of numerical superiority, but they also had developed a complex set of biases against Mexicans and Mexican Texans. In the Harrisburg District, these feelings became entrenched during the nineteenth century and would become the basis of Anglo-American views in the region for generations that followed. Generally negative, these attitudes contained a measure of ambivalence best illustrated by the roles of—and Anglo-Texan views toward—Lorenzo de Zavala and Juan Seguín.

Manuel Lorenzo Justiniano de Zavala was originally from Mérida, Yucatán. Well educated, widely traveled, a political author, and a liberal, Zavala was deeply involved in politics during the 1820s in the Mexican Constituent Congress, in the Mexican Senate, in the State of Mexico as governor, and as Minister of the Treasury under Vicente Guerrero. His interest in Texas dated at least from March 1829, when he was awarded an *empresario* contract to settle five hundred families there.

An ardent supporter of the Federalist Constitution of 1824, Zavala quarreled with General Antonio López de Santa Anna, then President of Mexico. Zavala relocated to Texas in July 1835, where he purchased a home for his family on Buffalo Bayou in the Harrisburg District and became active in the events of the Texas Revolution.

An orator in both English and Spanish, Zavala represented Harrisburg at the 1835 Consultation and at the Convention of 1836 at Washington-on-the-Brazos, where he signed the Texas Declaration of Independence. He was elected by the convention to be ad interim vice president of the Republic of Texas. He served in that capacity until mid-1836. Zavala died of pneumonia on November 15, 1836 and was buried in his family cemetery, which later became part of San Jacinto State Park. This leading Mexican statesman of the Harris County area has since been revered as a Texas hero and as a symbol of the Texas Mexican participation in the Texas struggle for independence. Some of Zavala's descendants still live in Harris County.

Occurring within sight of Zavala's home, the Battle of San Jacinto was perhaps the most important event of the revolution and certainly of major significance to the future of Mexican Texans. *Tejanos,* led by Captain Juan Seguín, played a key role in the San Jacinto campaign and the battle itself.

The story of Juan Seguín introduces the other, more prevalent side of Anglo-American attitudes toward Mexicans in Texas that would set the stage for the conditions of Mexican Americans in Houston.

The scion of an old Texas family, Juan Seguín was an implacable foe of General Santa Anna and the Centralists. Seguín was a political leader in San Antonio and always advocated good relations with the Anglo-Texans. He had an illustrious career in the revolution, where he sided with Jim Bowie, Stephen F. Austin, and William B. Travis. Raising a sizeable force of mounted men from the *ranchos* along the San Antonio River, Captain Seguín proved decisive in the rebel victory. The actions of Seguín and his men culminated at the Battle of San Jacinto, where most of the Ninth Company, Second Regiment Texas Volunteers, was made up of Texas-born *Tejanos.* This *Mexicano* unit represented the only company under General Sam Houston substantially composed of native Texans. In the thick of the fighting, Seguín's men helped ensure Santa Anna's defeat.

Like so many other Texans of Mexican heritage, however, Juan Seguín's sacrifices went underappreciated. As the population of the new Republic of Texas swelled with Anglo-American immigrants in the early 1840s, Seguín, back in his native San Antonio, faced unjust accusations of being a traitor to the cause of Texas. He was so ostracized by these newcomers that he fled the Republic to northern Mexico, where Mexican officials viewed him with suspicion. Scorned as treasonous by Mexico yet a victim of prejudice in Texas, Juan Seguín epitomized the unfortunate condition of many Mexican Texans during the latter nineteenth century.

The events of 1836 that so profoundly shaped the destiny of Mexican Texans also triggered the birth of the town of Houston and the inauspicious introduction of Houston's first Mexican residents.

In August 1836, a few months after the Battle of San Jacinto, John and Augustus Allen, two brothers from Brooklyn, New York, purchased several thousand acres of coastal prairie at the confluence of Buffalo and

Mexican prisoners from General Santa Anna's army helped to clear and drain the land to build Houston in late 1836.

White Oak Bayous, eight miles from Harrisburg. They mapped the property as a speculative town that they called Houston, in honor of the hero of San Jacinto, and offered the real estate for sale to the general public. The success of their venture came when the Texas Congress designated the site as the temporary location of the capital of the Republic.

The Allen brothers needed laborers to clear the land and build the structures that would house the fledgling government. They found some of those workers among the Mexican prisoners from the Battle of San Jacinto. Many of the several hundred prisoners, in lieu of being held captive on Galveston Island, were contracted to planters and settlers to work at skilled and unskilled jobs. Apparently, the Allen brothers obtained several of these men to clear and drain their town site.

These earliest Mexican workers became objects of curiosity to the other residents. Some of these former San Jacinto prisoners chose to stay in Harris County rather than return to their native land after being released.

Far removed from the main *Tejano* settlements, the Anglos of Houston manifested negative feelings toward people of Mexican stock. While they seemed to appreciate the qualities of Zavala and others, the shadowy side of their attitudes had been shaped both by their own heritage and by recent events. The violence of the Texas Revolution (which included the burning of Harrisburg by the Mexican Army), continuing border warfare between Texas and Mexico, and the Anglo-Americans' ingrained prejudice toward people of darker complexion guided many of their actions. As historian Arnoldo De León pointed out in his classic *They Called Them Greasers,* the Texas frontiersmen possessed an acute racism against people with Indian blood as well as a traditional suspicion and distrust of Spain and Catholicism, which they derived from their Northern European, Protestant backgrounds.

Because most *Mexicanos* and *Tejanos* were *mestizos* (a mixture of the Spanish and Mesoamerican Indian peoples) and professed the Catholic faith, they almost naturally became the targets of negative stereotyping in early Houston. This attitudinal legacy of the first half of the nineteenth century would profoundly affect later generations of Mexicans in Houston.

These pervasive feelings caused many Houstonians by the late 1830s to view these first few Mexican residents of the town, isolated and far from their homeland, with ridicule and scorn. Moreover, Houston produced two of the more vociferous anti-Mexican newspapers in Texas during the 1840s. The Houston *Telegraph and Texas Register,* under its editor Francis Moore Jr., considered Mexicans a "mongrel race, inferior even to negroes." The newspaper consistently portrayed Mexicans as backward and degenerate. Moore, who served as Houston's mayor in 1838–39, reflected the bigotry and chauvinism of many of his fellow citizens when he speculated that people of Mexican heritage were incapable of being true Texans (he himself was originally from Massachusetts). For Moore, Mexicans were defective, while "the term Texian [was] synonymous with that of American."

The other important Houston newspaper, the *Morning Star,* likewise touted the supposed superiority of Anglo-Americans over Latins and envisioned the conquest of all of Mexico by Anglo-Texans. It displayed the streak of early Anglo-Houston racism toward *Mexicanos* and helped foster prejudice in the Houston vicinity.

The number of Mexican inhabitants of Houston and the surrounding area remained relatively few until the latter part of the nineteenth century. The tax records of 1840 and the census of 1850 each have approximately a half-dozen individuals in the county with recognizable Spanish surnames. These few included people who lived and worked at various jobs in town or who owned land in the outlying area. Doubtless others dwelled in Houston, where, like many people in the town's fluid and mobile society, they picked up employment where possible without establishing a permanent residence. But just like their more-settled fellow Houstonians of Mexican descent, they contributed as best they could to the development of the rapidly growing town on the banks of Buffalo Bayou.

Eciquia Castro, ca. 1905, owned a café at 613 San Felipe Street. Her dignified bearing and hard work reflected the efforts of the founding generation of Mexican Houstonians. Photo courtesy of the Houston Metropolitan Research Center, Houston Public Library, Castro Family Collection.

CHAPTER THREE

Establishing an Urban Presence, 1880–1910

PEOPLE OF MEXICAN HERITAGE established themselves as a small but distinct part of the Houston population in the three decades prior to the Mexican Revolution of 1910. Numbering around two thousand people by 1910, they took their place as one of the city's recognizable ethnic groups. Mexican surnames and the Spanish language became permanent features of what was then called the "City of Magnolias."

Mexicans came to Houston in response to forces that transpired in Mexico, throughout the Texas Gulf Coast, and within the city itself. Worsening economic conditions south of the Rio Grande, the expanding railroad network and industry in Texas, and the emergence of Houston as a leading commercial and manufacturing center played direct roles in making Houston the destination of people of Mexican descent. These newcomers formed a population base that would later become a true urban ethnic community.

In the mid-nineteenth century, before the railroad networks turned Houston into a town of regional significance, Mexicans remained a negligible fraction of its population. A handful worked as cooks, housekeepers, laborers, or peddlers. By the 1870s, several Spanish-speaking individuals plied such trades as shoemaking and tailoring.

Mexicans migrated to Texas in increasing numbers during the mid-1880s to escape population pressures and worsening economic conditions in their homeland. The economic policies of President Porfirio Díaz, favoring a concentration of wealth, already produced hardship for working-class Mexicans. Some young men fled the mounting political turmoil and military impressment. The Texas-Mexico border proved permeable to immigrants coming north, each for their own reasons. They trickled into Houston because it was emerging as a dominant economic force in its region.

Between 1875 and 1890, Texas railroads significantly increased their miles of track, with Houston at the center of this expansion. This web of rail-line transportation made it possible for Houston to accelerate its commercial and manufacturing endeavors. Raw materials such as cotton, lumber, and hides from the interior of Texas passed through Houston on their way to market, and manufacturing enterprises such as textile mills and compresses, where Mexicans found employment, developed along Buffalo Bayou, Houston's waterway to the sea.

Mexican workers were involved in one of the earliest labor disputes in Houston's commercial nexus. Labor historian Robert Zeigler found that in late 1880, seventy-five Mexican workers were transported in to break a strike of black laborers at the docks of the Direct Navigation Company and related Houston industries, including cotton compresses and railroads. Such use of Mexican labor was common in Texas at the time, but apparently eleven of the *Méxicanos,* after hearing the complaints of the African Americans, actually refused to work.

Houston's Mexican population probably reached one hundred no sooner than the late 1880s, although numbers are difficult to determine. They took their place alongside other more traditional Houston ethnic groups of the nineteenth century, including blacks, Germans, Irish, and Italians. These early Mexicans comprised a fluid, transient population that possessed a broad range of skills and occupations, including bookkeepers, railroad workers, tailors, clerks, carriage drivers, barbers, iron molders, and common laborers. A few peddled Mexican foods at Houston's market square, while others operated neighborhood grocery stories. Vendors sold *tamales* on street corners and at stands. The first of several Mexican restaurants in Houston during the nineteenth century appeared around 1885, thus introducing Mexican cuisine to the palate of non-Hispanic Houstonians.

By the late 1890s, the trickle of Hispanic immigrants to the city became a steady flow. An adjusted computation of the 1900 federal census for Harris County suggests that the population of Mexican Houstonians stood at somewhere just below five hundred people in a city of over forty-four thousand. The majority were recent arrivals from Mexico, but some hailed from South Texas, and a few of the more enterprising Hispanics came from different parts of the United States, such as Florida and Louisiana. Houston had numerous small businesses owned and operated by people of Mexican descent and other individuals with Spanish surnames. A large portion of the young men worked for the railroad industry in the Southern Pacific shops and as section hands on *el traque* (track maintenance) in the principal railroad yards on the west, north, and east sides of town. Even a few peripatetic Mexican labor contractors came to Houston to secure such jobs in the outlying regions for their workers as cutting wooden posts and quarrying rock to help construct other parts of the economic infrastructure of modern Texas.

The living conditions of working-class Mexicans during the *Porfiriato* continued to deteriorate after 1900, and Texas remained a safety valve for thousands who chose to leave their homeland. Houston's economy steadily attracted them with jobs or rumors of jobs. The city began a federally subsidized improvement of its ship channel in order to become a deepwater port by 1914. This development, combined with the great hurricane of 1900, which permanently crippled Galveston as a rival, and the discovery of oil in East Texas and later in areas nearer to Houston, ensured that Houston would become the leading port on the Texas Gulf Coast. By 1910, the complementary development of railroads and the ship channel allowed Houston to tout itself as the city "where seventeen railroads meet the sea."

During the first decade of the twentieth century, the number of Mexican Houstonians would reach two thousand in a general population of seventy-eight thousand. The more fortunate held jobs as tradesmen or with the railroad as laborers. The use of low-paid Mexican workers in Houston had become so commonplace that there was a Mexican labor agent who contracted with local businesses and farmers in nearby agricultural regions for day laborers. Many Mexicans had small businesses, while others, no doubt in response to the chronic underemployment among Hispanics, continued to resort to peddling, selling *tamales,* and operating chili stands on Houston's back streets to sustain themselves. While Houstonians had inherited negative images of their new Mexican neighbors, they often remarked that the city's Mexican residents could be hard working, of sound reputation, and likeable.

Although these people who settled in Houston between 1880 and 1910 comprised little more than a collection of individuals and families, evidence exists of a Mexican American urban community. By 1910, some residential patterns became discernible. Mexican Houstonians had established themselves in scattered groupings across town near their places of employment, with the heaviest concentrations west of downtown and along Washington Avenue, near the shops of the Houston & Texas Central (Southern Pacific); to the north near the Missouri, Kansas, & Texas Railroad yards and the Texas & New Orleans (Southern Pacific) Railroad; and to the east of Main Street in the Second Ward near the International and Great Northern Railroad yards. Mexicans also found work in various cotton compresses located along the railroad lines and near the ship channel.

These areas were the scattered beginnings of Mexican neighborhoods that would expand to create Houston's North Side *Barrio* and *El Segundo*

Two brothers, Mauro and Paulino García, ca. 1905, came to Houston, the "City of Magnolias," from the state of San Luís Potosí seeking opportunity. Photo courtesy of the Houston Metropolitan Research Center, Houston Public Library, Castro Family Collection.

Barrio, where Mexican families and single men rented rooms in old homes that had been converted into apartments and rooming houses. There, also, small Hispanic businesses catered to the modest needs of the residents. Along with their places of employment, these rooming houses and business establishments may well have served as the initial locations of community association for Mexican Houstonians.

Perhaps even more telling evidence of formative steps toward creating a true community in these years came with the formation of the first known formal Mexican American organization in Houston. *El Campo Laurel,* a council of the Woodmen of the World (WOW), a benevolent society for mutual aid, was founded in the Second Ward on March 2, 1908. Under council commander Jesús Muñoz, Houston's *los hacheros* provided fraternal association and life insurance as security amid the urban milieu.

El Campo Laurel's founding members numbered approximately twenty men, some with wives and children and others single. They represented the spectrum of Mexican Houston and came from every part of town where Mexicans lived. Unlike cities such as San Antonio, Houston had no indigenous Hispanic traditions and offered immigrants no established

Earliest extant photograph of *El Campo Laurel*, Woodmen of the World, ca. 1920, founded in 1908 as the first Mexican American organization in Houston. Photo courtesy of the Houston Metropolitan Research Center, Houston Public Library, Joe Rodríguez Family Collection.

institutional support. Prior to *El Campo Laurel*, Mexicans in Houston relied on friends, neighbors, coworkers, employers, *la familia* (the traditional social unit), or the Mexican Consul for succor in times of emergency.

As historian F. Arturo Rosales first noted, the establishment of *El Campo Laurel* indicated that the Houston Mexican populace was not only sizeable but also had evolved a level of cohesiveness and identity. It became the parent organization of many Mexican American groups in the city as its members and their offspring generated other organizations during the next decades.

Historians Roberto Treviño and Arnoldo De León discovered that as early as 1907 the city's Mexican residents celebrated *Diez y Seis,* the traditional Mexican national holiday of September 16, at the Saengerbund Hall near downtown. In 1908, the celebration became more elaborate when a *junta patriótica,* presided over by John J. Mercado and including much of the leadership of *El Campo Laurel,* held a more formal affair at the Woodmen of the World Hall. They invited the Houston public to the festivities, which featured music and speeches about Mexican Independence and its hero, Father Miguel Hidalgo. The Mexican consul stationed in Galveston delivered one of the addresses. Approximately forty other Mexican residents from the Island City accompanied the consul to the event, thus illustrating the connection between the two communities.

Many of these recent arrivals had become accustomed to celebrating Mexican national holidays under the regime of Porfirio Díaz. Such festivities allowed Mexican Houstonians to reaffirm their identity amid their unfamiliar new conditions. As if to underscore the adaptability and acculturation of the Houston Mexican population to their new surroundings, during the 1908 celebration the audience was entertained with music that included the Mexican National Hymn and "Dixie."

As the "City of Magnolias," Houston had many decidedly "Old South" traditions that, in these years, had given rise to an elaborate annual celebration by the Anglos called "No-Tsu-Oh" ("Houston" spelled backward), which crowned King "Nottoc" ("cotton" spelled backward). Its equivalent in the African American community was "De-Ro-Loc" ("colored" spelled backward). No doubt these celebrations had an impact on the nature of Houston's initial *Diez y Seis* festivities, one manifestation of Houston's influence on its earliest Mexican residents.

Already, too, individuals became visible to the larger community. John J. Mercado and his son, John J. Mercado Jr., taught Spanish language at Houston High School and the Texas Business Institute, respectively, in 1910. Houstonians generally viewed the Mercados, originally from San Antonio, as the "first family" of local Hispanics, especially for their efforts to introduce Anglos to Mexican culture. Almost daily, Houstonians saw the handiwork of sign-painter Joseph M. Gómez, the town's most successful Spanish-surnamed businessman. Ecequia Castro, her mother, and other relatives had emerged as well-known purveyors of Mexican food and representative of the families that established themselves as the founding generation of Mexican Houstonians.

Houston's city government likewise recognized the presence of the fledgling Mexican community through embryonic provision of services. Treviño and De León found that in 1908, the police department hired an officer specifically assigned to duty within the Mexican populace.

The strength of this pre-1910 generation stemmed from the families and their informal interactions. Families and close friends provided support and comfort and transmitted Hispanic culture to Houston; the first Mexican holiday celebrations and religious gatherings took place privately in people's homes. Special breakfasts and other meals in private houses among friends and acquaintances also served as focal points for group interaction. Eager to associate with people of a similar background, families on weekends often waited at Houston's railroad depots on the chance that they would meet Mexicans just arriving. As true urban pioneers—in small businesses, as employees, and as neighbors—Hispanics were an increasingly integral part of the cosmopolitan port city.

By 1910 the number of Mexican residents (which had steadily grown since 1880) was obvious to anyone who came to town. John Milsaps, a Houston diarist who had watched the city grow for nearly half a century, wrote in November 1910 of a new trend no doubt evident to all its inhabitants. While strolling along a side street near downtown, Milsaps "heard the Spanish tongue . . . making me think of Matamoros. Mexicans are numerous in Houston," he noted.

Members of the singing and theatrical group of Magnolia Park, ca. 1928, founded by Feliciano Chairez, were symbols of the growing Mexican American influence in Houston between 1910 and 1929. Photo taken in the studio of Houston photographer Jesús Murillo. Courtesy of the Houston Metropolitan Research Center, Houston Public Library, Chairez Family Collection.

La Colonia Mexicana in Houston, 1910–1929

HOUSTON'S MEXICAN AMERICAN POPULATION became a truly viable urban community between 1910 and the Great Depression. In response to the outbreak of the Mexican Revolution and attracted by new economic developments in Houston during these years, large numbers of people of Mexican descent came to make Houston their home, extending the fledgling Hispanic neighborhoods and creating new *barrios* where none had existed before.

As their numbers grew to approximately six thousand in 1920 and to around fourteen thousand five hundred in 1930, Mexican Houstonians evinced a remarkable degree of tenacity and adaptability. They formed a network of grassroots organizations and institutions that allowed them to begin to express themselves collectively and to determine their own destiny as a people.

The dire social and economic conditions in Mexico during the three previous decades finally culminated in the Mexican Revolution of 1910. Historian Arturo Rosales, in his perceptive analysis of this formative period, notes that after a temporary hiatus in Mexican immigration to Houston caused by the outbreak of hostilities, the fighting and economic disruption forced thousands to come to the Bayou City, far surpassing the numbers that had arrived during the preceding decades.

The majority of the newcomers to Houston by 1920 had escaped the revolutionary struggles of northern Mexico to settle in the west, north, and east sides of Houston. By 1920, the *manzanas* (city blocks) *de Mexicanos* multiplied in the First, Second, Fifth, and Sixth Wards. *El Segundo Barrio* largely consisted of Mexican Americans. Immigrants had likewise turned a portion of Magnolia Park, an independent municipality established in 1908 along the Ship Channel near Harrisburg, into a newly created *barrio*. These areas contained a healthy mix of Mexican Americans from South Texas.

Ramón and Delfina Villagomez, ca. 1914, from Morelia,
Michoacán, were representative of the many people who
came to settle in Magnolia Park and Houston. Photo courtesy of the Houston Metropolitan Research Center, Houston Public Library, Villagomez Family Collection.

Because of the increasing numbers of Mexican residents in Houston,
the Catholic Church sent Oblate priests to found a parish in 1911 and
address parishioners' spiritual needs. Located in the midst of the Second
Ward's *Méxicano* population, the wooden frame church constructed in
1912 was named Our Lady of Guadalupe after the patron saint of Mexico.
Directed by a priest from Spain named Estéban de Anta, it became a center of the Houston *colonia.*

The Sisters of Divine Providence established Our Lady of Guadalupe
parochial school in 1912. The nuns' school filled a need since Houston
public schools seemed insensitive to the concerns and culture of *la colonia* and showed meager interest in educating Mexican children. In 1915,
Sister Benitia Vermeersch became principal and through her dedication
ensured the school's effectiveness in helping local children obtain their

Our Lady of Guadalupe Church, ca. 1912–14, with its congregation, priests, and nuns, 60 Marsh Street at Runnels Street in *El Segundo Barrio*, was constructed in 1912 as the first Mexican American church in Houston. Photo courtesy of the Sisters of Divine Providence.

The second structure of Our Lady of Guadalupe Church after its consecration on September 2, 1923, with original building visible in right background, now stands as perhaps the most historic building in Houston's Hispanic community. Photo courtesy of the Houston Metropolitan Research Center, Houston Public Library, Villagomez Family Collection.

eighth-grade diploma. The parish further consolidated in 1923, when a more permanent red brick church was built. Together, Our Lady of Guadalupe church and school provided two key institutions for the emerging *barrios*. It represented a complex, as historian Roberto Treviño notes, that demonstrated the parishioners' self-reliance, vitality, and ability to carve out "their space in the Bayou City."

As the decade progressed, with the opening of the Houston Ship Channel as a deepwater port and the outbreak of the First World War, Houston's economy boomed as never before. Hearing of possible jobs by word of mouth and through the efforts of *enganchistas* (labor agents), Mexican workers and their families flocked to Houston. So many Mexican people had settled in the North Side–Fifth Ward area near the railroad yards that by 1920 the Methodists had established a Mexican Methodist Church there with the Reverend J. M. de los Santos as pastor.

As their numbers increased, Mexicans' cultural events became more visible. A lively *Diez y Seis* celebration took place in 1917 under the sponsorship of *comités parióticos* made up of North Side and *El Segundo Barrio* residents, much enlarged over those of the previous decade. By the late 1910s, the Mexican inhabitants of Magnolia Park also became active in such community affairs. Their involvement expanded by the establishment in 1919 of *La Sociedad Mutualista Benito Juárez,* a mutual aid society that offered its membership life insurance and a social outlet. This popular organization rented a hall (*salón*) on Navigation Boulevard where it held many well-attended cultural functions. Under its first president, Elías Ramírez, *Mutualista Benito Juárez* stressed retention of Mexican traditions and grassroots self-improvement. It sought members from everywhere and helped to make Magnolia Park into a center of Mexican Houston culture.

Such community organizations addressed some of the problems that the people of *la colonia* faced. Many recent arrivals lived in shoddy, unpainted two- and three-room frame houses. In some cases, more than a dozen people lived in one room. Many of the families of railroad laborers lived for a time in freight cars, and everyone suffered from the elements and bad hygiene. Such deprivation naturally caused a myriad of health problems. Pneumonia, influenza, tuberculosis, diarrhea, and a host of other maladies were prevalent. It seemed as if every family suffered an unnecessary death of a child or older relative.

Mexican residents of the Second Ward turned to Rusk Settlement House for help by the late 1910s. Rusk Settlement, established in 1909 as an agency of the Houston Settlement Association, extended a variety of services, from English classes to recreational activities to first aid from visiting nurses. It became a favorite meeting place for the people of *la colonia*

as it hosted small *fiestas* and other cultural affairs. It was not until 1924 that
a health clinic (the so-called Mexican Clinic) was opened in the Second
Ward. Begun by the Catholic Church, it provided medical care to many in
la colonia and, in 1947, was renamed San José Clinic.

Difficult conditions in the Bayou City caused by an acute recession
in 1921 did not lessen the flow of immigrants. As thousands more came
north, displaced by the continuing turmoil south of the Rio Grande, many
stayed in Houston.

By 1923, Houston entered a time of prosperity and rapid growth. *La
colonia* to some extent shared in these flush times as immigrants from
Mexico and other parts of Texas more than doubled its population.
Despite the immigration laws of 1917 and the more stringent ones of 1924
and 1929, by 1930 approximately fourteen thousand five hundred Mexican
Houstonians lived in a city of three hundred thousand.

Like those who had come before them, these immigrants sustained
immeasurable hardship on their journey to Houston in search of peace and
opportunity. They came by train, by automobile, and on foot, often working at odd jobs along the way before finally reaching the Bayou City. Their
numbers even included a sprinkling of ex-soldiers from the defunct revolutionary armies of Generals Francisco Villa, Venustiano Carranza, Emiliano
Zapata, and others. Many of the men found openings with the railroads—
jobs that provided an economic base for their families and community.

Other men found jobs as cooks, busboys, dishwashers, and waiters in
Houston hotels, restaurants, and cafes; as bakers and butchers; as custodians
and construction workers; as store clerks and salespeople; and in a range of
different employment. In the late 1910s, for example, Jesús Gutiérrez and his
son, Patricio, both played in the early Houston Symphony. Patricio was an
exceptionally talented concert pianist who had an important influence on
the musical scene as an instructor. Those young women who worked outside the home often found jobs in small scale, piece-work manufacturing
industries near their places of residence.

During the 1920s, the ranks of *la colonia's* middle class expanded as
many Mexican businessmen, entertainers, teachers, doctors, artists, and
photographers, especially from west-central Mexico, came to Houston in
response to the deteriorating conditions in their native land. Historian
Rosales suggests that many of these refugees initially settled in San Antonio, where established Mexican communities allowed them to practice
their professions, before ultimately settling in Houston.

By 1928, a handful of young medical doctors, such as Jesús Lozano,
Angel Leyva, A. G. González, and Luis Venzor, had located in the Bayou
City. Not only did they become community leaders, but they also delivered

badly needed medical attention to their neighbors. Speaking Spanish and charging below the going rates, these doctors were accessible to the wage earners of *el pueblo Mexicano.*

Houston's Hispanic business community came into its own in the 1920s. With thousands of potential customers on hand, enterprising people opened a wide range of commercial establishments. Although trade flourished wherever Mexicans resided, many of these firms were concentrated east of Main Street in a several-block strip centering along the 1800 block of Congress Avenue. From the 1920s until World War II, this area was considered the downtown shopping district of Mexican Houston and included furniture stores, bookstores, cafes, a drugstore run by a Mexican pharmacist, barbershops, a hotel, doctors' offices, commercial photography studios, and other businesses. A principal example of such entrepreneurship were José, Socorro, Felipe, Jesús, and María Sarabia, four brothers and a sister from a small town in Guanajuato who by the 1920s were operating several successful enterprises along Congress Avenue. (María and her husband, Raúl Molina, ultimately became prominent Houston restaurateurs.)

The Alamo Furniture Company (Francisco Gabino Hernández, proprietor) was one of the thriving businesses in the 1800 block of Congress Avenue near downtown Houston during the 1920s. Photo courtesy of the Houston Metropolitan Research Center, Houston Public Library, Gabino Family Collection.

La colonia's business and professional elite were joined by other members of the community who, unlike the greater portion of Mexican Houston, enjoyed upward mobility during the decade of the 1920s. A few young men and women held white-collar positions with Anglo companies. A handful of Spanish-surnamed students attended Rice Institute, including Primitivo L. Niño and Francisco Chairez, who earned degrees as engineers in 1928. Their educational achievements were touted by *el pueblo* as examples for Mexican American youth to emulate.

During the 1910s and 1920s, the influx of Mexican immigrants to Magnolia Park resulted in that area becoming the largest Houston *barrio* by 1929. They had settled there after 1910 to help with ship channel–related construction. Soon, however, they began to purchase lots in the immediate area to build homes with the money they had managed to bring with them or on reasonable terms with their earnings. Located along the ship channel, Magnolia Park quickly became ringed with industrial development, decreasing its marketability to Anglos. Eager to sell the property, land agents financed lots to Mexican families who wanted to own homes and be near their places

Hispano Americana bookstore, ca. mid-1920s, with owners José (*left*) and Socorro (*right*) Sarabia was located at 1811 Congress Avenue. Photo by Houston photographer Luís Suárez. Courtesy of the Houston Metropolitan Research Center, Houston Public Library, Sarabia Family Collection.

Francisco Chairez, Rice Institute graduate, 1928, represented the Hispanic community's pride in high school and college attendance dating from the earliest times. Photo courtesy of the Houston Metropolitan Research Center, Houston Public Library, Chairez Family Collection.

of employment. On these parcels, the newcomers, many of whom had carpentry skills learned in their homeland, built single-family frame dwellings of superior quality and created a tightly knit community.

Residents of Magnolia Park, which Houston annexed in 1927, had access to downtown by streetcar line and close proximity to ship channel jobs. Many found employment in construction, in the compresses, and in other large-scale industry as well as in smaller businesses doing such work as cleaning plants, bakeries, and piece-work manufacturing.

East of Magnolia Park, in places such as Pasadena and Baytown, other pockets of Mexican habitation took root when oil companies built refineries during the 1920s near the ship channel toward Galveston. In most cases, the refining companies utilized Mexican laborers who lived in tents and other forms of temporary housing near the work sites. Many made the coastal region their permanent home. By mid-decade the residents of Pasadena had founded *La Sociedad Mutualista Miguel Hidalgo.* Such mutual aid societies formed an emerging network of community groups in Harris County.

Magnolia Park residents contributed to the proliferation of *colonia* institutions in the 1920s. In 1926, local residents established the Immaculate Heart of Mary Church, Houston's second predominantly Mexican Catholic Church. It soon became the spiritual center of Magnolia Park, adding to its growing sense of neighborhood cohesion. Magnolia Park likewise produced several Protestant groups, including Mexican Presbyterian and Pentecostal congregations. The Presbyterians, under Reverend José Hernández, were particularly visible in Magnolia Park.

When Houston annexed Magnolia Park, it enlarged Lorenzo De Zavala School, originally established in 1920 as the "Mexican School" for Spanish-speaking children in the lower grades of that area.

Mexican Houstonians reveled in their sports associations. *El Club Deportivo Azteca* fielded soccer and baseball teams using the finest players from various neighborhoods. These sports groups, especially baseball, received support from Mexican-owned businesses. The Alamo Furniture Company, under its owner Francisco Gabino Hernández, sponsored the *Los Alamos* baseball team for several years. Perhaps the most successful *colonia* baseball team, also believed to be among the earliest, was the Mexican Eagles. During the early 1920s, the Eagles played Anglo-American teams from across the city, hardly losing a game. The Eagles received much attention from the leading Houston newspapers for their ability on the diamond and for their reputation as one of the best teams in Houston.

Mexican American young people in Houston founded such social clubs as the Merry Makers at Rusk Settlement House. The Roseland Steppers (more commonly known as the Rolling Steppers), a dance club begun by a group of dapper young men, was probably the most exciting group in the early 1920s. It sponsored citywide dances on a regular basis, giving young adults a wholesome social outlet.

Founded in 1924, *El Club Cultural Recreativo México Bello* became the most lasting of these early social organizations. Drawing its membership from all parts of Houston, *México Bello* provided the best in formal dances, picnics, and an assortment of well-publicized events. Under its long-time president Ramón Fernández, it gave Houston's *colonia* social

A Houston soccer team, ca. 1927, represented one of a variety of sports activities in the local Hispanic community. *Front row, left to right:* Antonio López, Charley Farías, and F. Rodríguez; *second row, left to right:* José Juárez, Gaspar Castillo, and Cebero Ayala; *back row, left to right:* Santos Nieto, Salvador Tellez, A. Navarro, Augustine Castillo, and Benny Lee. Photo courtesy of the Houston Metropolitan Research Center, Houston Public Library, Augustine Castillo Family Collection.

elite that became a "who's who" in Mexican American Houston and consciously sought to present the mainstream Houston community with the best features of Mexican culture.

La colonia offered only limited possibilities for political association during the 1920s. Although most of the new arrivals had fled political strife in Mexico and maintained a low profile in Houston, some residents were less reluctant to assert themselves. One such individual was Fernando Salas A., a native of Chihuahua and an owner of a jewelry business. Arturo Rosales found that Salas and Frank Gibler, an Anglo newspaperman sympathetic to the Mexican community, began *La Asamblea Mexicana* in 1924 in reaction to continued police brutality, a constant feature of life for Mexicans in Houston. *La Asamblea* established some rapport with the police, voiced opposition to the local Ku Klux Klan, and tried to deal with the many difficulties faced by the Mexican students in Houston public schools. Salas, Gibler, Ramón Fernández, Isidro García, and others made Mayor Oscar Holcombe aware of community concerns, and he in turn recognized the Mexican presence in the city with regular visits to Mexican American functions. Most *colonia* residents began to support Holcombe's many campaigns for re-election as the dominant political personality in the Bayou City during these years.

Cultural life in Houston's *pueblo Mexicano* blossomed in the 1920s. Guadalupe Church boasted a theater that featured plays performed by both locals and visiting acting troupes. In 1928, *Mutualista Benito Juárez* constructed a new *salón* (including a theater) that served a similar function in Magnolia Park. A well-known theatrical group from Magnolia Park, founded by Feliciano Chairez, performed for community gatherings across the *colonia*.

The September 16 and *Cinco de Mayo* (May 5) celebrations brought together members of the various clubs and organizations. The continuing activity of the *comités patrióticos* served in many respects as a unifying force for the community as they selected their yearly queens from among the young ladies of Houston and Magnolia Park. Some of Houston's early Hispanic photographers recorded the especially nice *Diez y Seis* affairs held at the *Salón Juárez* in 1924 and 1928 and at the Houston City

Members of *La Asemblea Mexicana* (Houston's first Hispanic political organization) and other participants at a *fiestas patrias* celebration in Magnolia Park in 1928. Founder Fernando Salas A. stands ninth from left. Photo by Houston photographer José Belmonte. Courtesy of the Houston Metropolitan Research Center, Houston Public Library, Mr. and Mrs. Fernando Salas A. Collection.

Elvira Gómez, Queen of the *Diez y Seis de Septiembre* festivities in Houston in 1924. Photo courtesy of the Houston Metropolitan Research Center, Houston Public Library, Melesio Gómez Family Collection.

Auditorium in 1926. During the 1920s, professional photographers from the Mexican American community such as Luís Suárez, José Belmonte, and Jesús Murillo began to open commercial studios and produced stellar images of Hispanic subjects.

The most exciting cultural entertainment for Mexican Houston started, however, in 1927 with the opening of *El Teatro Azteca* by the Sarabia Family on Congress Avenue. The *Azteca* succeeded the Hidalgo Theatre that had functioned for a short time just a few blocks away. The *Azteca* was the first successful commercial theater for Mexicans in the Bayou City and featured both live performances and motion pictures. It hosted well-known acting companies and singers. Vaudeville groups such as *Los Hermanos Areu* became especially popular with local audiences. The *Azteca* was a favorite spot in *la colonia* as people crowded in to see the numerous Spanish-language celebrities who traveled the entertainment circuit in the United States.

At all the events held in the emerging *barrios,* music played a crucial role. Mexican Houstonians, having brought their appreciation and talent for music as part of their cultural baggage, utilized their clubs and groups to form bands. The presence of several distinguished music teachers who had fled Mexico especially fostered these musical groups. Strolling Mexican guitarists and singers entertained Houston North Side residents in neighborhoods near the railroad yards. Years later, older Anglo Houstonians fondly recalled the presence of these troubadours whose nighttime serenades enhanced an air of community congeniality. Our Lady of Guadalupe church formed a nineteen-piece band to play at bazaars and other church functions. Individual musicians joined company bands, performed with singing clubs, or began dance bands of their own. On at least one occasion, the Southern Pacific Railroad Band had to cancel a performance because its Mexican American members had to play with other groups for *Diez y Seis* functions, an indication of the strength of its Hispanic participants.

The community especially appreciated the existence of dance bands. The Apolo Six was one such popular group. *Los Rancheros* quickly emerged

El Teatro Azteca at 1809½ Congress Avenue (pictured on July 15, 1927, probably opening night) was the first successful Spanish-language theatre in Houston and a cultural hub of the local Hispanic community. Photo courtesy of the Houston Metropolitan Research Center, Houston Public Library, Sarabia Family Collection.

Los Rancheros Orchestra, photographed in Galveston in 1930, began in Houston in 1926. *Left to right:* Octavio Estrada, trumpet; Jesús Garza, accordion; Lorenzo Garza, guitar; Andres Ortíz, drums; Antonio Bañuelos, piano; and Frank Tijerina, Rosendo Velázquez, and Juan Velázquez, saxophones. Photo courtesy of the Houston Metropolitan Research Center, Houston Public Library, Lorenzo Garza Collection.

as perhaps the best remembered of the early Mexican American dance bands in Houston. This *orquesta* (orchestra or "big band") was organized in 1926 by the brothers Lorenzo and Jesús Garza, recent arrivals from Matamoros. To gratify their local audience, the talented band's repertoire of songs included both Mexican and American favorites. In his later years, Lorenzo Garza remembered proudly that if someone could almost hum the tune, *Los Rancheros* could play it.

La Orquesta Típica Torres widely popularized classical Mexican music. Founded and conducted by Albino Torres, a professional musician from Mexico City, the string orchestra became extremely popular with audiences from the *barrios* to the "ritziest" areas of Anglo Houston. A troupe of local Mexican singers and dancers often performed with the orchestra. Their featured vocalist, Mimi Ypiña, was a highly celebrated Houston opera singer. The group even had a radio program that broadcast its music across the Texas Gulf Coast and earned its members a letter of congratulations from the President of Mexico. Torres himself would become one of the most accomplished piano instructors in the Bayou City.

The Houston *colonia* during the 1920s produced several Spanish-language newspapers for the first time. Musician Jesús Gutiérrez published *El Anuciador.* Blaso Alonso Capatillo, who reportedly later lost his life in an unsuccessful rebellion in his native Mexico, edited one called *La Tribuna.* Rodolfo Avila de la Vega published the weekly *El Tecolote,* which became the longest running and most popular. A well-known figure around town, Vega often gathered the news himself, much as the other publishers of these early papers did. The Sarabia family published and Lorenzo Yañez edited *La Gaceta Mexicana,* a literary magazine that featured essays, poetry, and society news. These periodicals carried numerous advertisements of local Hispanic businesses. In addition to San Antonio's *La Prensa,* several newspapers from Mexico that circulated in Houston, and a Scripps-Howard publication called the *Houston Press,* the small local papers helped to fill the news and information needs of *la colonia* and kept their readership in touch with community events.

The residents of *la colonia Mexicana* in Houston needed the spiritual bolstering that its celebrations, newspapers, churches, and clubs provided. They also appreciated the succor they received from many of their sympathetic employers, individuals with whom they formed life-long associations. Too often, however, they suffered from urban dislocation, discrimination at the hands of many within mainstream society, and random violence. Chronic poverty also troubled their community, even in the midst of the relative prosperity of the late 1920s.

Most of the adults of *la colonia* in Houston felt their ties with Mexico deeply in these years, and many dreamed of one day returning when conditions there improved. For most of them, this desire would never materialize. As their children became Americanized, the parents found that they could never return to their homeland. Still, they stressed their "Mexicanness," what historians like Arnoldo De León have termed "*Lo Mexicano.*" Arturo Rosales poignantly explains that the immigrants regarded their homeland as "*México Lindo*" (Beautiful Mexico), a nostalgic sense for what good things they had left behind. Despite their ambivalences, however, these recent arrivals remained and made the best of their situation.

Even before the stock market crash of 1929, job opportunities for Mexicans in Houston had started to dwindle and the steady numbers of Hispanic newcomers were less able to locate employment. In many ways, the hard times of the Depression began early for Mexican Houstonians. Nonetheless, the approximately fourteen thousand five hundred Mexican residents in Houston had established themselves as a viable, functioning community of several distinct neighborhoods between 1910 and the eve of the Great Depression. This ethnic community would indelibly mark Houston, contributing its labor to many sectors of the booming economy and lending its cultural flavor to the entire city.

Sergeant Macario García receiving the Medal of Honor from President Harry S. Truman in 1945. García had moved to the Houston area from Mexico during his youth and after the war became a highly visible symbol of Mexican American participation in World War II. Photo courtesy of the Houston Metropolitan Research Center, Houston Public Library, John J. Herrera Collection.

CHAPTER FIVE

Hard Times and War, 1929–1945

THE PERIOD BETWEEN THE ONSET of the Great Depression and the end of World War II was a time of great stress and reorientation for the Houston Mexican American community. The relative prosperity of the previous decade gave way to general unemployment, deprivation, and suffering. In response, during the 1930s a curious phenomenon called "repatriation" occurred, a process by which a substantial portion of the Houston *colonia* returned to Mexico.

However, in-migration and a steady birthrate actually increased Houston's Mexican population so that by 1940 it consisted of twenty thousand people. Simultaneously, a new group of Mexican Americans raised in Houston came of age by the late 1930s—providing fresh leaders who would increase their community's influence in the city. With the advent of World War II, large numbers of these young Hispanics joined the American war effort, unequivocally linking their destinies with that of the United States.

When the Depression began, opposition to foreigners on relief or holding jobs escalated and a campaign began across the country to remove Mexican nationals either through deportation or voluntary repatriation. Ultimately, five hundred thousand Mexicans left the United States, half of them from Texas. In Houston, as in other regions, the repatriation of Mexican residents was encouraged as a means of alleviating unemployment problems.

Even though Houston, with its economy based on the oil industry and ship channel, did not suffer as severely as most other areas of the nation, by 1930 the city was experiencing economic woes. In the Mexican American community, businesses that had prospered in the 1920s began to fail and a frightening percentage of the workers began to lose what jobs they held.

By 1931, general unemployment had increased precipitously. Relief agencies in Houston such as the Community Chest were very soon over-extended and running out of money to help the jobless. The general policy of federal and state relief agencies in Houston, as elsewhere, was to bar aliens and non-residents from local assistance and public jobs. Houston's prevailing attitude was that employment in local relief projects should be reserved for white citizens.

Most Mexicans simply may not have expected assistance from the larger society or feared deportation if they did report to relief facilities. For example, of the 150 Houstonians who registered on the first day of a city-instituted work program in 1931, none were Mexicans.

Between 1929 and 1933, the Immigration Service conducted raids on construction job sites in the Houston-Galveston area that resulted in the deportation of hundreds of Mexican workers. Even legal residents became fearful of such activities and tried to stay as inconspicuous as possible in the workplace. Nativist sentiments among the general Houston populace supported these expulsions.

In response to these dire conditions, a "voluntary" repatriation movement developed in Houston. The Mexican Consul reported in 1930 that 333 Mexican families registered as leaving Houston for Mexico. During the last six months of that same year, 895 families from Houston recorded their departure to Mexico at Laredo. Daniel Garza, the Mexican Consul assigned to Houston, began organizing the return of a number of Houston residents to Mexico in January 1931. With some financial help from local *mutualistas*, Garza relocated approximately fifty families to the Don Martín Irrigation project, promising them government land.

A rather pathetic photograph, captioned "Mexicans Being Shipped to Homeland," appeared in a local newspaper in May 1932. It showed a truck-load of Mexican Houstonians of varying ages waving goodbye. The door on the truck bore the inscription *Comité Mexicano Pro-Repatriación Houston*. An accompanying article detailed the activities of the *comité*, which was chaired by Houstonian Bartolomé Casas. The committee assisted the repatriates by obtaining donations for their transportation to the border and apparently organized the relocation of several groups.

Rusk Settlement House proved especially active in assisting these repatriation efforts. During the summer of 1933, thirty-two people departed for Laredo from Rusk. In accepting and assisting these returnees, the Mexican government required them to sign affidavits declaring their intention to remain as permanent residents of Mexico. During the late 1930s, Mexican officials spoke at community gatherings and in homes to foster repatriation. The enticement included the promise of land and the lingering feelings that Mexico, as their *patria*, offered an alternative to their present desperation.

Ramon Beteta, Under Secretary of Foreign Relations for the administration of President Lázaro Cárdenas, toured the United States in April 1939 to recruit Mexicans to return to their homeland. Concentrating most of his efforts in Texas, Beteta visited Houston, where he offered land, the possibility of public jobs, and easy credit for houses, livestock, and other necessities. Beteta spoke at public meetings in Houston and even visited individual homes. He worked with the Mexican consulate to arrange for families' departure and the transportation of their possessions south. Over 150 people from the Houston area departed for a government colony at the end of May 1939.

Historian Marilyn Rhinehart has estimated that at least two thousand Mexican Houstonians, approximately 15 percent of *la colonia's* population in 1930, left during the Depression. The lack of records makes exact numbers impossible to ascertain, but certainly the entire process represented an experience that profoundly touched the community. This dislocation strained the fabric of *la colonia*.

Despite the repatriates' hope that in Mexico, on free land, they might escape their sorry plight, they underwent no little measure of distress and trauma. Most tragic were the children who accompanied their parents to Mexico because in many cases they were American born. Many children became separated from their parents due to the financial and familial hardships of the move. Some stayed with friends or relatives for years at a time. Children also lost their fluency in English and missed crucial years of schooling during this disruption. Others, having lived their first ten or twelve years in the United States, found it difficult if not impossible to adjust to their parents' homeland.

Although the Mexican government tried to resettle the repatriates, many of the returning Houstonians felt severely disappointed at what they encountered. Substandard living conditions, poor wages, and crop failures in the depressed Mexican economy frustrated their attempts to adapt.

The experience of several hundred Mexicans from Houston who settled in the village of Cameron near Nuevo Laredo in the state of Nuevo León was representative of the repatriates' many difficulties. Their efforts at cotton farming on the rocky, arid land were frustrating, and in the late 1930s a storm destroyed many of their homes and turned the water and soil of the area salty. Most of the residents of Cameron soon moved to the Eighteenth of March government colony. The remainder had little to ensure their livelihood. As Houstonian Juan Carrión, a survivor of this experience, commented many years later, they had "nothing . . . but mesquite, cactus, and snakes."

A meeting of Houston's *La Sociedad Mutualista Obrera Mexicana,* July 2, 1944.
Founded on February 21, 1932, the *Obrera Mexicana* dealt with many commu-
nity problems of this difficult time. Photo courtesy of the Houston Metropolitan
Research Center, Houston Public Library.

While many of the repatriates reestablished a life in Mexico, others fil-
tered back across the border to Houston, disappointed with their stay yet
doubly wary of the perils of life in the United States.

The community that they rejoined in Houston also struggled. Members of the Mexican *colonia* tried to take care of their own during the crisis
through family, friends, and mutual aid societies. In 1932, for example, a
group of residents in the Second Ward came together to bury an indi-
gent neighbor killed in an accident. This group established *La Sociedad
Mutualtista Oberera Mexicana* in response to this immediate need. In that
same year, *El Campo Navidad,* another chapter of the Woodmen of the
World, was established in Houston with Arnulfo Cárdenas as Council
Commander.

Organizations such as *El Campo Laurel* and *Benito Juárez,* along with
the newly created *Obrera Mexicana* and *El Campo Navidad,* directed all
their efforts toward the survival of their membership, but their resources
were limited. In 1932, the members of *Mutualista Benito Juárez,* no doubt
because they were unable to meet expenses, lost the hall they had built
four years before. The *Diez y Seis* and *Cinco de Mayo* celebrations were
decidedly smaller because available funds to promote such activities were
sadly lacking.

A handful of local welfare organizations, such as Rusk Settlement, the

Methodist Church's Wesley Community House established in 1930, and the Neighborhood House of Magnolia Park Settlement founded in 1933, did what they could to meet some of the people's needs. The nuns of Our Lady of Guadalupe School provided free meals for their students as the parish assisted its poorest families in various ways.

Many businesses that had once given the community a commercial fabric closed down. Even the number of newspapers decreased to one or two, and they published less frequently. Abject poverty increased dramatically. The most wretched examples existed in the slum housing area in the Second Ward known as *El Alacrán,* reputedly named for the numerous scorpions that came into the run-down, shotgun houses from the banks of nearby Buffalo Bayou. In *El Alacrán* was the notorious Schrimpf Alley, a side street that exemplified the most extreme case of poverty and crime in Mexican Houston.

Still, the community experienced an overall population growth and development amid these difficult times. While many had left, others migrated or relocated to Houston, especially from rural Texas, where the Depression was even more acute. Also, families that remained gave birth to children, adding to the populace.

The winners of a raffle given by grocer Ernesto Rodríguez in Magnolia Park, December 25, 1935, stand with their prizes, including a bicycle, a heater, a radio, a handbag, sacks of flour and other food, and a heifer. Photo by Houston photographer Gregorio Cantú. Courtesy of the Houston Metropolitan Research Center, Houston Public Library.

Mexican American employees of the Lone Star Bag and Bagging Company, Houston, celebrate Christmas at work in 1939. Photo courtesy of the Houston Metropolitan Research Center, Houston Public Library, Joe Rodríguez Family Collection.

In this period of the late 1920s and early 1930s, Mexicans began to settle in the residential area just north of Liberty Road and west of Lockwood Drive near the Englewood Yards of the Southern Pacific Railroad. These yards included a creosote wood-preserving plant, and the residents referred to their neighborhood as *El Crisol,* so strong was the odor that permeated the air. A few small Mexican American–owned shops, cafes, and other businesses sprouted in *El Crisol* to cater to the families of the railroad workers. Hard-pressed for extra money, young people in the area started social clubs such as *El Club Lázaro Cárdenas* (named for the reformist president of Mexico in the 1930s) as inexpensive recreation. They also gravitated to Our Lady of Dolores (Sorrows), the new Catholic Church for that expanding Mexican *barrio.*

Mexican Americans throughout Houston found what jobs they could in those fields that traditionally gave them employment. They even participated to some extent in labor unions, particularly within the united Textile Workers of America and the international Longshoremen's Association along the ship channel.

Those young people who were American citizens took advantage of certain New Deal programs such as the Civilian Conservation Corps (CCC), the National Youth Administration (NYA), and the Works Progress

Administration (WPA). They were exposed through these government jobs to the broader Anglo community as many of them went to faraway places, especially with the CCC, to labor on projects designed to improve parks and other public facilities. Altogether, such agencies proved to be a positive experience for many. The money they earned supported their families in the *barrios,* and when World War II broke out, these experiences prepared them successfully for life in the military. These important Depression-era programs, along with other examples of sensitivity toward working people shown by the administration of Franklin Delano Roosevelt, established the tradition of allegiance to the Democratic Party among the Mexican Americans of Houston. It became clear to the young people of the community that to participate fully in American society, citizenship and assertiveness were necessary.

Such assertiveness became most evident among the generation of Mexican Houstonians reaching adulthood during the 1930s. Firmly rooted in their community, these younger men and women sought to expand their horizons and activities beyond what their elders had envisioned. Either born in the United States or having been children during their families' migration to Texas, they linked their destinies more closely with the United States and wanted to participate more fully in its society. They provided the vanguard for the new direction of advancement of Houston's Mexican American community.

Mainly through the activity of this younger generation, two important new organizations—Council 60 of the League of United Latin American Citizens (LULAC) and the Latin American Club of Harris County (LAC)—formed during the mid-1930s. LULAC, begun in Corpus Christi in 1929, took root in Magnolia Park in 1934 when Manuel Crespo, a young immigrant from Spain; Mariano Hernández, originally from San Antonio; and Elías Ramírez initially organized a council.

LULAC Council 60 hosted the 1935 LULAC state convention and the 1937 national convention. These events brought a great deal of positive notice to the Houston Mexican American community from the local media, as Houstonians saw Mexican Americans meeting to discuss their roles in American society. By using the term "Latin American" as opposed to "Mexican" for self-designation, both LULAC and LAC sought to identify more fully with their surroundings and avoid the onus attached to the latter term by Anglo-Texan society.

LAC formed in 1935 when a group of men wanted a club more centrally located near downtown Houston. Headed by John Duhig, probably Houston's first Mexican American attorney, Manuel Crespo, John J. Herrera, Juvencio Rodríguez, and Felix Tijerina, LAC took on more political overtones as it

Houstonian Tony Martínez with the Civilian Conservation Corps (CCC), popularly called the "Tree Army," ca. 1940. Photo courtesy of the Houston Metropolitan Research Center, Houston Public Library, Carmen Cortes Collection.

Mexican American musicians in a Works Progress Administration (WPA) orchestra, Houston, 1935, were hired by the federal government to provide jobs and community entertainment. Photo by Houston photographer Gregorio Cantú. Courtesy of the Houston Metropolitan Research Center, Houston Public Library, Monico García Collection.

A private dinner, ca. 1930s, at *La Consentida*, a popular café owned by Melesio Gómez at 1708 Washington Avenue in the Sixth Ward and the location for many community activities during the Great Depression. Photo courtesy of the Houston Metropolitan Research Center, Houston Public Library, Melesio Gómez Family Collection.

endorsed candidates and ambitiously tried to register the city's many Latin voters. Both groups held poll tax drives and sought to educate the community in their duties and responsibilities as American citizens. However, their outspoken advocacy of Mexican American rights represented their most significant pursuit.

LULAC and LAC members tried to encourage Houston employers to cease discrimination against Mexican Americans. Young Mexican Americans in search of employment found that many businesses in Houston would not hire them because of their ethnicity. Plants in the Harrisburg industrial area, adjacent to the *barrios,* made a practice of posting signs that read "No Mexicans Hired Here."

In 1938, LAC and LULAC became embroiled in a controversy at city hall that underscored the posture of this new generation of Mexican American Houstonians. In response to a proposal to pay a group of water department employees, half of whom were Mexican Americans, for the San Jacinto holiday, a city commissioner was quoted as asking why "Mexicans" should be paid for celebrating the day they were "beaten."

Pointing out that they, too, were American citizens, LAC and LULAC immediately spearheaded a protest in front of city council against such prejudicial humor, an effort that garnered a great deal of local publicity and brought the commissioner much embarrassment.

On a more serious note, in 1937, the two groups were outraged by the case of two Houston policemen who had been involved in the death of a local resident named Elpidio Cortéz. Cortéz had died while in the custody of the officers, who were then indicted for his murder. Their trial and eventual acquittal received much play in Houston. To members of LAC, LULAC, and the Mexican American community at large, the Elpidio Cortéz case served as another example of how law enforcement officials in Texas abused their people.

LAC and LULAC of Magnolia Park combined into LULAC Council 60 of Houston by 1939 with the purpose of making Mexican Americans a more integral part of Houston society.

Concurrent with the development of men's organizations during the 1930s, young Mexican American women formed clubs in an effort to express their interests and concerns. In 1935, Ladies' LULAC Council 14 started in Magnolia Park. It sponsored dinners and raffles to raise money for community activities. Founded in the early 1930s, *El Club Femenino Arco Iris* held bazaars in Magnolia Park. *El Club Femenino Chapultepec,* a young women's group under the auspices of the YWCA, tried to raise the civic consciousness of Mexican Americans as well as educate the city's Anglo community about Mexican culture. A group of young women formed *Club Social Terpsicore* in 1937 to hold dances and other social affairs. By 1940, civic and social organizations such as *Club Selva, Cielito Lindo, Club Orquidea,* and *Club Femenino Dalia* drew their membership from aspiring young women of *la colonia.*

Regardless of the hard times, the community continued to produce a number of organizations. Clubs included both the 1910s and 1930s generations, whose overlapping membership in these different groups helped to maintain the interconnectedness of the community.

El Club Recreativo International emerged in the 1930s to rival, at least for a time, *El Club Cultural Recreativo México Bello.* Other groups included *Club México, Club Recreativo Fiat,* and *Club Artistico Mitla.* The various clubs came together in the late 1930s to establish a comprehensive organization called *La Conferencia de Sociedades Mexicanas de Houston* under Manuel Crespo as president. The assemblage became *La Federación Regional de Sociedades Mexicanas y Latinoamericanas de Houston,* part of a larger statewide effort to better the condition of all people of Mexican descent living in Texas. Mexican Consul Luis Duplán acted as advisor to

Officers of *Club Femenino Chapultepec*, 1936–37. Such groups represented the emergence of young Mexican American women in urban areas like Houston. This composite photo by Gregorio Cantú was common to the era. Courtesy of the Houston Metropolitan Research Center, Houston Public Library, Carmen Cortes Collection.

the regional federation. The Mexican Consulate consistently aided Houston's Spanish-speaking residents, especially prior to World War II, when a large percentage of them were Mexican citizens. During his tenure in Houston, Duplán was particularly involved in such affairs.

By 1940, the community's businessmen had recovered sufficiently from hard times to found the Houston Mexican Chamber of Commerce under the directorship of Carlos Ortiz, formerly of Los Angeles, who had established one there before moving to the Bayou City. The chamber had seventy-two members and, like most community groups, accepted the participation of both citizens and non-citizens.

The community's longstanding interest in sports manifested itself in the creation of a Latin American Sports Council in 1940. Mexican Houstonians during the late 1930s and early 1940s were especially involved in boxing, producing several notable contenders in the amateur and professional ranks. This new involvement in Anglo-American sports was highlighted in March

The men of *Club Cultural Recreativo Mexico Bello,* 1932, at their gala New Year's Eve "Black and White" ball. *Mexico Bello* ranked as perhaps the leading Hispanic organization in Houston of its time. Photo courtesy of the Houston Metropolitan Research Center, Houston Public Library, Mr. and Mrs. Isidro García Collection.

Circulo Femenino Mexico Bello (Mexico Bello Ladies' Club), ca. 1936, from which many of the most influential women's community voices would emerge. Photo courtesy of the Houston Metropolitan Research Center, Houston Public Library, Mr. and Mrs. Felix Tijerina Collection.

1945, when Houstonian Gilbert García won the national championship for his weight division in the Golden Gloves tournament held in Chicago.

The membership of *Club Tenochtitlán,* made up exclusively of high school students in the late 1930s, represented the first generation of Mexican American pupils produced by the Houston school system. These youngsters were among the first Mexican Americans in the city to experience true biculturalism. While they celebrated their Mexican heritage, they held few illusions about ever living in Mexico. By 1940, a Mexican American Boy Scout troop functioned in Houston, which, again, underscored how younger people worked their way into mainstream society.

During the early 1940s, some young men of the Houston community sported zoot suits, an expensive "hip" style of dress marked by drape-shape pants with reet pleat, ankle-tight cuffs, and long ornamental chain, a baggy coat, and wide-brimmed flat hat. Although a fad among other ethnic groups as well, it came to be popularly associated with Mexican American young people at the crossroads of both cultures.

A segment of Houston's Mexican American youth, however, was not able to deal constructively with the many problems faced by their community. *Colonia* residents suffered chronic juvenile problems with which they attempted to deal through community committees specifically for youth. These committees pushed for more park space, recreational facilities, educational improvements, and other types of social outlets.

To meet these deficiencies, the city opened Hidalgo Park in Magnolia Park in 1934 and also upgraded Fifth Ward's Hennessey Park in 1939. In 1940, Ripley House of the Neighborhood Centers Association opened in the heart of Second Ward, bringing wholesome pastimes and social services to people of all ages. Ripley House would thereafter remain a constant feature in the East Side.

Youths alienated by the deprivations of the era and the urban environment formed so-called *pachuco* gangs in neighborhoods on the fringes of society. The *barrios* produced such groups as the Black Shirts from the Second Ward and the *El Alacrán* gang, whose members supposedly sported a tattoo of a scorpion. Another Latin gang called the Long Hairs hailed from Magnolia Park and gained a great deal of notoriety during the 1940s.

Every neighborhood had a gang that jealously guarded its turf. Violence often erupted between the various groups on the streets, at dances, and during other community events, especially in the early 1940s. Mexican Americans referred to the Fifth Ward, for example, as the "Bloody Fifth," so frequent did beatings, shootings, and stabbings occur among rival gang members. Police often arrested these young men and women because of their violent behavior as well as for their less-than-subservient attitudes toward law enforcement and other Houston authorities.

In mid-1944, much against the advice of the leadership of the Mexican American community, the Houston Police Department assigned three officers as a so-called "Latin American Squad" to deal specifically with the *barrios*. Author Luis Rey Cano, in his analysis of this episode, explains that LULAC had responded to the city's proposal for such a squad in late 1943 by holding a community meeting attended by several hundred concerned Mexican Americans.

The meeting protested creating the special force because it singled out Mexican Americans as a "special problem." This gathering called for the city to promote more recreational and educational outlets as well as job training programs to combat juvenile delinquency. The community did what it could to alleviate the problems of its young people and calm the tension in the city through neighborhood committees comprised of members of the various clubs.

The coming of World War II quickened the pace of Mexican American involvement in Houston's political process and further cemented *la colonia's* destiny to that of the United States. Former members of LAC and other activists established the Latin Sons of Texas, an organization of native born and naturalized American citizens that garnered publicity in Houston by touting Roosevelt's defense policy as war approached in 1941. The Latin Sons fostered civic action, planned poll tax drives, and held neighborhood functions where they endorsed candidates for local and statewide elections. By 1940, as prewar patriotic fever rose, the Pan American Club under President Edward Flores also hosted political rallies that sought to raise Mexican American political consciousness.

When the United States entered the war, Mexican American Houstonians served in large numbers in every branch of the armed services. Entire neighborhoods seemed to be depopulated as their young men were either drafted or volunteered for duty.

Families compiled scrapbooks of the many newspaper items mentioning local Mexican American residents in every theater of action. One story featured six sons of the same parents, at least one in each branch of the service. Many from the Houston area, like Medal of Honor winner Macario García of Sugar Land, were highly decorated for heroism on the battlefield.

In 1942, the city was reminded starkly of its Mexican American participation when Joe Padilla, Houston's first casualty, was buried with full military honors by the American Legion. Raised in the North Side *barrio*, Padilla had joined the Navy before the war and died in the Indian Ocean.

Houston's first casualty in World
War II was Joe Padilla, a Mexican
American from the North Side.

The experience of the war profoundly touched the lives of most Houston Mexican Americans and gave shape to the direction of the community's future. To a much greater degree than any of the New Deal programs,
the armed services broadened the horizons of the young men who served,
most traveling beyond the confines of Houston for the first time and asso-
ciating with Anglo-Americans from regions of the country where prejudice against Mexican Americans was negligible.

Mexican American servicemen fought overseas for democratic principles that they would want applied to their own lives when they returned.
Parents whose sons went to distant lands felt deeply their investment in
the society with which they previously had little in common. This proved
especially the case when Mexican American war dead came home for
burial, when families received letters from their young men from foreign nations, or when families learned that their sons had been killed,
wounded, or taken as prisoners of war.

On the home front, organizations across the spectrum in Mexican
American Houston affirmed their commitment to the war effort. Many
groups sold war bonds and participated in other patriotic activities in
Houston to help the cause. LULAC adopted the slogan "Remember Pearl
Harbor" and touted Mexican Americans in uniform. In 1942, John J.
Herrera and a LULAC delegation began placing a wreath at the San Jacinto

Houstonian Ted Garza, standing at the grave of his brother Gilbert
in Holland, where the latter was killed in 1944 during the allied
invasion of Europe. This image was taken to inform and console
family members back home who were mourning the loss of their
loved one. Photo courtesy of the Houston Metropolitan Research
Center, Houston Public Library, Navarro Family Collection.

Monument to celebrate the *Tejano* company in Sam Houston's forces in
that 1836 battle, thus connecting Mexican Americans with valor for Texas
and the United States. Even in their Mexican national holiday festivities
during the war years, the *comités patrióticos* took up the theme of American victory in Europe and the Pacific.

Mexican Americans also began to work in the war-related industries as activists such as John J. Herrera and LULAC officers utilized the
President's Committee on Fair Employment Practice to see more job
opportunities open up in the various refineries and shipyards, calling
into question longstanding discriminatory hiring practices of Houston
businesses. Herrera worked especially closely with Dr. Carlos E. Casta-
ñeda, a scholar from the University of Texas and member of the President's Committee, to rectify such grievances.

War industry employment added much-needed income to the community and alleviated many of the conditions of the Depression. The supply

of these jobs attracted thousands of Mexican Americans to Houston from across the Southwest and contributed to the unparalleled growth of the *barrios* during the 1940s. In addition to the income, these wartime positions gave Mexican Americans added skills and confidence to be utilized when peace resumed.

Despite the difficulties faced by the Mexican American community in Houston, by the mid-1940s a sense of optimism had replaced the desperation of the early 1930s. Mexican Americans gained new recognition. For example, in 1941, at the urging of Mexican American representatives from the local International Longshoremen, LULAC, and other Houston community organizations, Harris County hired Carmen Cortes, a local resident, as the first Mexican American in a white-collar position at the courthouse. The empanelling of Houston jeweler Fernando Salas A. in August 1944 as the first Mexican American member of a Harris County Grand Jury also represented a symbolic gain that would set a precedent for the decades that followed.

Their efforts at home and in the armed services gave Mexican Houstonians a strong sense of participation in a society they felt they helped to build and preserve. Although still faced with a myriad of problems, Mexican Americans began to feel the potential of inclusion rather than the absolute bitterness of exclusion. Altogether, the struggles, hardships, and gains of the 1930s and early 1940s strengthened and consolidated the Houston Mexican American community in preparation for the important postwar era.

Queen of the September 16, 1948 festivities Julia Aleman (*right*) and members of her court at the Houston City Auditorium, expressive of the enthusiasm of Mexican Americans in the postwar period. Photo courtesy of the Houston Metropolitan Research Center, Houston Public Library, Melesio Gómez Family Collection.

CHAPTER SIX

Latin Americans in Postwar Houston, 1946–1958

THE YEARS IMMEDIATELY FOLLOWING WORLD WAR II were as expansive for Mexican Americans in Houston as they were for the rest of the city. The economic boom created by the war continued apace and Houston's population skyrocketed. Technological advances and the petrochemical industry, which tied Houston to world markets, required greater numbers of workers and ensured a proliferation of businesses.

Although many of their problems continued, the war had generally acted to improve things for Mexican Americans in Houston. During these postwar years, their expanding middle class, their increasing educational attainment, their broadened horizons as a people, and their general ability to cash in on the relative affluence of the era allowed more of them to insinuate themselves into broader activities.

The Mexican American community saw its numbers parallel the fantastic growth of the rest of the city. By 1950, approximately forty thousand Mexican Americans resided in Houston and its environs. The process of assimilation into Houston's society, incipient by the late 1930s, accelerated in the postwar period as Mexican Americans (most commonly called "Latin Americans" in this era) evidenced an increased familiarity with their urban environment. True to the direction established in the previous two decades, the community leaders of the 1950s saw their future squarely in the United States. They fought discrimination more openly as they struggled to share in the prosperity of a society buttressed by their sacrifices and hard work.

Mexican American veterans who came back to Houston after the war wanted to do more than pick up where they had left off. After all, their wartime experiences had raised their horizons and consciousness. They wanted the equality that they felt they had earned by risking their lives in a war against the specter of racial supremacy.

The conditions that they found in Texas, however, reawakened their old feelings of uneasiness. Even in their service uniforms, many were not allowed to enter segregated public facilities such as movie houses and restaurants. Regardless of their status as veterans, the policy of refusing service to Mexicans continued. This practice seemed especially prevalent in the small towns around Houston: Richmond, Rosenberg, Wharton, New Gulf, and others.

Houston's Mexican Americans were sharply reminded of this situation when Macario García was refused service at a café in Richmond, a few miles south of Houston, in September 1945. García, of Sugar Land, had been the much-publicized recipient of the Medal of Honor for heroism in Germany the year before and would come to symbolize the plight and contributions of Mexican American veterans of World War II.

While such discrimination usually took more subtle forms in Houston, it nonetheless comprised a part of everyday life for the average *barrio* resident. Some cases in Houston were as blatant as those in the nearby small towns. One café near downtown, infamous among the Latin Americans as a principal offender, displayed its "No Mexicans or Dogs Allowed" sign until the war's end and refused to serve even Mexican American ex-servicemen who came in for refreshments.

Mexican Americans in Houston would no longer tolerate such conditions. LULAC Council 60 became especially active in the advocacy of Macario García's case and in the fight to reverse such discriminatory practices as it rallied local Mexican American clubs, organizations, businesses, and individuals to support its efforts.

Although not an avowed political organization, LULAC in Houston quickly emerged as the most important advocate for Houston's Mexican American community in this period. The LULACs, most of whom belonged to the Democratic Party, articulated the general concerns of Houston's Mexican Americans since they also belonged to many other organizations and understood the needs of the community.

Almost as the opening salvo for Mexican American rights in the postwar period, LULAC Council 60 hosted the national LULAC convention in the Bayou City in 1946. As with the 1937 national convention, Houston LULACs in 1946, such as John J. Herrera, Rudy Vara, Dr. John J. Ruíz, Joe Castillo, Fernando Salas A., Isidro García, Frank Brett, Adolfo Martínez, Felix Tijerina, Philip Montalbo, Ernest Villareal, and Joe Luna, brought Houston media attention to this event and its efforts to publicize the contributions and potential of Mexican Americans in this society. In the postwar era, LULAC leaders immediately enlisted Anglo sympathizers in positions of authority.

Officer Raúl C. Martínez (*left*), mid-1950s, recognized as the first uniformed Mexican American officer in the Houston Police Department. Martínez would later become a highly respected Harris County Constable. Photo courtesy of the Houston Metropolitan Research Center, Houston Public Library, G. T. Valerio Collection.

Houston LULACs and Mexican Americans in general attacked problems on all fronts. They sometimes gained their point, as when in 1947 they worked with influential city officials to abolish the so-called Latin American squad in the Houston Police Department (HPD) (although the idea would be revived periodically).

Another significant milestone came in 1950 when LULAC helped persuade the HPD to hire its first uniformed police officers of Mexican descent. In that year, Raúl C. Martínez and Eddie Barrios entered the Houston police academy, ending a longstanding practice of employment discrimination by the city. By 1958, fifteen Latin American officers served in the HPD and an equal number in the Houston Fire Department. Although only a small percentage of the forces, the Mexican American presence in public jobs would continue to increase, especially under such progressive Houston mayors as Roy M. Hofheinz and Lewis W. Cutrer.

In the late 1940s, Mexican American Houstonians also accelerated their efforts to involve their community in the political process. Voter participation among Mexican Americans in Houston was pitifully low in the late 1940s. In response, community organizations encouraged people to pay their poll tax, although they objected to a tax that discouraged poor people from voting. The short-lived Pan American Political Council began in 1948 and tried to raise Latin American political awareness, a goal that had existed since the 1920s.

In the postwar years, the community also identified the educational system as a primary issue for Mexican Americans. On the state level, LULAC tried to abolish the widespread practice of segregating Mexican American children in Texas schools. In 1948, the courts in the case of *Minerva Delgado* v. *Bastrop* called for a halt to this practice, although as scholar Guadalupe San Miguel Jr. has pointed out, the decision did not see uniform enforcement across Texas.

On the local level, Houston Latin American students faced great difficulty. Most attended less-than-adequate schools in their own neighborhoods. Dr. John J. Ruíz and LULAC Council 60 worked with the Houston Independent School District (HISD) to improve the school facilities in predominantly Mexican American areas and tried to deal with the sporadic youth gang problems that again surfaced in the early 1950s. LULAC and other organizations worked to raise money for scholarships so that students could complete their high school education. Graduating from high school still represented a notable achievement for Mexican Americans in Houston.

The GI Bill of Rights was an educational boon for the community as it allowed veterans the opportunity of a college education. An unprecedented number of local people entered college, especially at the University of Houston, where they could study for a profession.

Simultaneously, the Houston Mexican American community expanded its middle class. Although some migration from Houston to places such as Los Angeles, Chicago, and Detroit in search of industrial jobs occurred, the Houston economy offered unprecedented opportunities. Also, in this postwar period, Mexican Americans began to succeed more effectively within the entrepreneurial mainstream of Houston. Opening businesses in service-related sectors, Mexican Americans again rode the wave of prosperity as they had during the 1920s.

With this relative improvement, new organizations developed that combined the traditional *colonia* flavor and the new postwar approach. For example, in February 1948, Mariano Rosales Ypiña, an employee of Southern Pacific who had come to Houston from Mexico in the early 1920s, and David Casas, a popular restaurant owner, founded *Club Familias Unidas*. Composed mainly of North Side residents, *Familias Unidas* functioned principally to provide a wholesome social atmosphere for youth and their parents in response to the social dislocation of the times.

La Moderna Grocery & Meat Market in Magnolia Park, early 1950s, with propri-
etors Tomás Flores and Frederico Cantú, in a family snapshot that reflected the
spirit and prosperity of Houston's postwar Mexican American business community. Photo courtesy of the Houston Metropolitan Research Center, Houston
Public Library, Tomás Flores Family Collection.

Club Recreativo de Veteranos formed in 1947 with an active membership of approximately seventy-five young ex-servicemen, mostly from
Houston's East Side. In 1949, the club became a chapter of the American
GI Forum under the direction of individuals such as Benito R. Herrera,
Richard Ante, and Oscar D. Ochoa. The GI Forum, originally founded
in Corpus Christi by Dr. Hector P. García, advocated for Mexican American issues in much the same vein as LULAC. Many of the members
also took part in Houston LULAC, since LULAC, with its dynamic local
leaders and junior council, operated as the more significant group in the
Bayou City.

The predominantly Hispanic Port Houston Lions Club became active
in the civic affairs of the community during the 1950s. It functioned as one
of the largest Lions Clubs in the Gulf Coast area and assumed a major role
in organizational matters.

Women's groups continued to operate as well. In May 1949, the Young
Women's Christian Association (YWCA) opened a Mexican American
branch in Magnolia Park. By 1952–53, the Magnolia Park Mothers' Club
was established and maintained a high profile in the area over the next
decade. During the late 1940s, Ladies' LULAC Council 22 organized in
Houston, succeeding the moribund Council 14 of the 1930s. In conjunction

Junior LULACs of Houston, ca. 1952. *Left to right:* Rudy Rodríquez, Consuelo Velásquez, Roy Rodríguez, Frank Urteaga, Petra Cisneros, Ben González, Rachel Cisneros, and Jimmy Zepeda. Photo by Bob Fernández. Courtesy of the Houston Metropolitan Research Center, Houston Public Library, Alfred J. Hernández Collection.

Ladies LULAC Council 22, 1955. *Seated left to right:* Mary Alice Palacios, Carmen Cortes, Elida Flores, Virginia Ochoa, Hilda Vázquez, Marcella Sosa, and Mary Louise Herrera; *standing left to right:* Carmen López, Minnie Chapa, Susie González, Julia Martínez, Luz Morales, Dora Patino, Ofelia Quintero, Julia Rodríguez, and Emma Flores. Photo courtesy of the Houston Metropolitan Research Center, Houston Public Library, Carmen Cortes Collection.

with Men's Council 60, the Ladies' LULAC entered an active period of community self-help programs. These newer groups seldom sought the advice of the Mexican Consul, as had been the practice before the war.

The census of 1950 revealed the drastic problems that these community organizations battled. Poor housing ranked among the worst. Generally, *barrio* residents lived in overcrowded conditions, with a high percentage lacking such basics as indoor plumbing. Census statistics reflected the continuing deterioration of the already decayed Mexican American sections of Houston's inner city. The Houston Housing Authority tried to reverse this trend with public housing projects. In 1953, the most wretched *El Alacrán* slums were cleared to make way for the construction of the Susan V. Clayton Homes, which would provide low-cost housing in the Second Ward.

As of 1950, although community leaders and public officials advocated and pursued education for Houston Hispanics as never before, actual attainment for Mexican Americans still averaged several years less than the city's norm.

Although the census revealed many problems, potential existed as well. In 1950, the Houston area's forty thousand Mexican Americans represented roughly 5 percent of the city's population, their numbers having doubled over the previous decade. Averaging twenty years of age, the Mexican Americans of Houston consisted, as a group, of much younger people than the rest of the city, and a larger percentage of them were unmarried than in the general population. The overwhelming majority included American citizens, most born in the United States and thus more familiar with their urban surroundings than previous generations.

By the 1950s, Houston's Latin Americans still resided in the north and east sides of town but were expanding their geographic boundaries. Like the rest of Houston, they became suburbanized. In particular, by 1950, Mexican Americans had moved into the Linndale and Denver Harbor subdivisions on the north side of town. The El Dorado subdivision of Wallisville Road developed in the mid-1950s as perhaps the quintessential Latin American subdivision of this period, with street names such as Aguila, Saltillo, Coahuila, and San Pedro. It even boasted its own *Diez y Seis* celebration by the end of the decade.

As the people moved into the suburbs, Mexican American businesses followed their clientele. The original downtown business district on Congress Avenue, which had dwindled since the Depression, decayed beyond recognition. Even the *Azteca* Theater ceased to exist by 1957, although the location continued to operate under another name for a few years more.

Its former customers more frequently chose to attend English-language movies and patronized the shopping malls, which mushroomed during the 1950s.

Culturally, the Houston Latin Americans of the late 1940s and 1950s reflected their exposure to and acceptance of the trends of mainstream society as well as the preservation of their Mexican roots. While much has been written of Mexican American assimilation in these postwar years, and although the Houston environment acculturated people to a greater degree than many other areas in the state, in actuality the city's Mexican Americans remained remarkably bicultural.

Those members of the community who were a generation or two removed from their Mexican origins usually remained bilingual, learning the Spanish language at home. The Mexican national holidays of *Cinco de Mayo* and *Diez y Seis* continued to be celebrated in grand style. One of the more impressive of these festivals took place in September 1948 at the City Auditorium downtown. In a celebration reminiscent of those of previous decades, the young people who participated that year elected their *Diez y Seis* queen and reminded the Bayou City of the Mexican presence.

The Mexican influence in Houston was perhaps most triumphantly displayed in 1952 when Cantinflas (Mario Moreno), Mexico's most famous comedian, gave reportedly his first performance in the United States to a capacity audience of Hispanics at the Sam Houston Coliseum. During the 1940s and 1950s, other Mexican entertainers toured through Houston, drawing large crowds.

Houston's Mexican American music reflected the biculturalization of these years. Rock and roll bands coexisted with *conjuntos* in the city. Mexican American dance bands such as *Alonzo y Sus Rancheros* responded to their audiences' tastes by playing American "big band" numbers as well as *la música ranchera* in their popular nightclub, *La Terraza*. The band's female accordionist and vocalist, Ventura Alonzo, ranked among the most talented musicians on the Gulf Coast.

Johnny Velázquez and his Valley Serenaders and the orchestras of such bandsmen as Gaston Ponce, Henry Tovar, Baltazar Hernández, Johnny Martínez, Tommy Flores, Kiddo Zapata, Lalo Ruíz, and many others in the mid-1950s entertained their Houston audiences with mambos and cha-cha-chas in a variety of dance halls that catered especially to Mexican American crowds. A generation of Mexican Americans went to dances at the Pan American Nite Club, the Paladium, the Blossom Heath, the *Tropical,* and numerous other night spots across Harris County.

Popular local orchestra *Alonzo y Sus Rancheros* with Alonzo Alonzo, drummer; Ventura Alonzo, vocalist and accordionist (*front standing*); Frank Alonzo, guitarist; and Frank Alonzo Jr., bass fiddle, at their *La Terraza* night club in the 1950s. Photo courtesy of the Houston Metropolitan Research Center, Houston Public Library, Frank and Ventura Alonzo Collection.

Dance at the Pan American Nite Club, 1705 North Main Street, late 1950s, probably the most popular of the many entertainment spots across the city. Photo courtesy of the Houston Metropolitan Research Center, Houston Public Library, G. T. Valerio Collection.

Houston's well-known *Eloy Pérez and the Latinaires*, late 1940s. *Front row, left to right:* Sisto Pérez, Locadio Pérez, Eloy Pérez, and Felipe N. Pérez. Photo courtesy of the Houston Metropolitan Research Center, Houston Public Library, Eloy Pérez Family Collection.

Perhaps the most widely known of the big bands from Houston was Eloy Pérez and the Latinaires. The youngest of four brothers in the original orchestra founded after the war, saxophone player Eloy Pérez toured his group across Texas and the Southwest, influencing an entire generation of Mexican American musicians.

In the postwar years, Houstonians also began to take special note of particular individuals who personified the aspirations of the Latin American community. Among these remarkable people was John J. Herrera, attorney and civic activist, who caught the public eye when in 1947 he ran for the state legislature, launching the first viable (although unsuccessful) political campaign by a Latin American Houstonian. Herrera's family lineage in Texas dated from the Canary Islanders who had settled San Antonio during the 1700s. In 1952, Herrera won election as national president of LULAC and helped to expand that organization throughout the Gulf Coast and southwestern United States. While he often worked effectively with members of the Anglo establishment, Herrera did not hesitate to directly confront cases of discrimination. His work in LULAC and advocacy of Mexican American civil rights became legendary in the community. A participant in several important court cases, Herrera probably is best remembered for his part (along with attorneys Carlos C. Cadena and Gus C. García of San Antonio) in the case of *Pete Hernández* v. *the State of Texas*. The Hernández case, decided by the U.S. Supreme Court in 1954, barred the exclusion of Mexican Americans from petit and grand juries.

Funeral home director Manuel Crespo emerged as another outstanding civic leader in the 1950s. He had been active in groups before the war and had served as a detective with the HPD during the 1940s. He became

John J. Herrera, Houston attorney, civil rights leader, and LULAC national president, 1952–53. Houston's mayor Oscar Holcombe is seated behind Herrera. Photo courtesy of the Houston Metropolitan Research Center, Houston Public Library, John J. Herrera Collection.

Manuel Crespo, civic leader and owner of Crespo Funeral Home, receiving an award as the founder of the Port Houston Lions Club, mid-1950s. Photo courtesy of the Houston Metropolitan Research Center, Houston Public Library, G. T. Valerio Collection.

Ladies LULAC members Josephine López (*left*) and María Reyna (*right*) advertising their annual charity ball at Houston's Shamrock Hotel in 1954. Photo courtesy of the Houston Metropolitan Research Center, Houston Public Library, Alfred J. Hernández Collection.

Felix, Angelina, and son Joe Morales during the 1950s. The Moraleses were
civic leaders and the owners of Morales Funeral Home and radio station KLVL.
Photo courtesy of the Houston Metropolitan Research Center, Houston Public
Library, Felix and Angelina Morales Collection.

the primary mover in such postwar organizations as the Port Houston
Lions Club. María Reyna, businesswoman and community leader, played
an enduring role in Mexican cultural events in this period. She was instrumental in Latin American involvement in the March of Dimes, the drive
against tuberculosis, and numerous other charities. She spearheaded
many of the *comité patriótico's* annual celebrations of Mexican national
holidays.

Felix and Angelina Morales started Houston's first Mexican American–
owned radio station, KLVL (*La Voz Latina*), in 1950 to give the community
what it lacked previously—a broadcasting voice. They provided airtime on
KLVL to Mexican Americans who needed to reach a larger audience with
important information. KLVL also played Latin music for the thousands
of Spanish-speaking listeners eager for familiar tunes. The Morales couple
originally came from San Antonio, founded a successful funeral home in
the Second Ward, and had been leading Mexican American entrepreneurs
in Houston since the 1930s. Their son, Joe, as a young adult in the 1950s,

Janie and Felix Tijerina, Houston entrepreneurs, civic leaders, and philanthropists. Photo courtesy of the Houston Metropolitan Research Center, Houston Public Library, Mr. and Mrs. Felix Tijerina Collection.

assisted them in their businesses and became a well-known media personality. As historian Chrystel K. Pit perceptively notes, the enterprises of the Morales exposed much of Houston to Mexican American and Mexican immigrant language and values.

Alfred J. Hernández, a young attorney, also came into his own as a force in civic affairs. Having come to Houston from Mexico with his family as a child, Hernández received his American citizenship in Europe while in the armed services during the Second World War. The embodiment of the "GI Generation," Hernández attended the University of Houston and the South Texas College of Law and assumed a place among the few Hispanic lawyers in town in 1953. He took his cue from associates, including John J. Ruíz, John Herrera, and others, who had been active since the 1930s. He stood out as a capable orator in both English and Spanish and quickly became a leader in several important organizations, especially LULAC.

Perhaps the most publicized Mexican Americans in Houston, however, were Felix and Janie Tijerina, owners of Felix Mexican Restaurants. By the late 1940s, local media identified the Tijerinas as the de facto spokespersons for Latin American Houston.

With his effervescent, congenial personality, Felix Tijerina, an immigrant from northern Mexico during the 1910s, emerged as the Mexican American version of the traditional boosteristic Houston entrepreneur and the paradigm of the postwar Latin American. Felix and Janie involved themselves in a host of Latin American and Anglo organizations. With Council 60 as his base and such loyal lieutenants as Alfred Hernández, Felix Salazar, Sammie Alderete, and others, Tijerina became LULAC national president in 1956. Under his direction, LULAC initiated the "Little School of the 400" in 1957 as a pioneer effort in Mexican American education. The program intended to teach Spanish-speaking preschool children four hundred basic English words so that they could deal adequately with the first grade. In this manner, its advocates reasoned, Mexican American children would not fall behind in their early school years,

Postwar LULAC Council 60 leadership, 1955. *Standing left to right:* Gabriel Ramírez, Philip Montalbo, Felix Tijerina, Sammie Alderete, Ernest Equía, and Arnold Quintero; *seated left to right:* Alfred J. Hernández and Gilbert Gómez. Photo courtesy of the Houston Metropolitan Research Center, Houston Public Library, Mr. and Mrs. Felix Tijerina Collection.

become discouraged, and ultimately drop out at the alarming rate that characterized the Texas Mexican community at the time.

Tijerina and LULAC established the pilot projects in the Texas towns of Ganado and Edna in 1957, and by the following year they had spread to other places in the state. The overwhelming majority of the project's pre-schoolers went on to successfully finish the first grade, a dramatic contrast to the appalling failure rate of children who did not receive such instruction.

The Little School of the 400 was consistent with LULAC's traditional emphasis on education as a primary focus for Mexican American advancement. Tijerina's own non-confrontational approach in dealing with the dominant society represented a principal tactic of the late 1940s and 1950s, especially during the Eisenhower years. He received much of his support from Anglo humanitarians, such as his good friend and fellow Rotarian R. E. Bob Smith. In 1959, through the help of such legislators as L. DeWitt Hale of Corpus Christi and Governor Price Daniel, Tijerina persuaded the parsimonious Texas State Legislature to adopt and fund the concept as the Preschool Instructional Classes For Non-English Speaking Children.

Tijerina and LULAC worked to spread the program across the Southwest. It became a forerunner for Project Head Start established under the administration of Lyndon B. Johnson, whose own experiences with teaching Mexican American children reinforced the government's commitment to the program. "Tijerina's schools," as they came to be known, also received publicity from such national legislators as the U.S. senator from Texas Ralph Yarborough.

Felix Tijerina's approach made Houston a focal point of state and national attention on Mexican American issues. Such periodicals as the *Saturday Evening Post* and *Time* magazine featured articles on Tijerina and the plight of Latin American education.

As LULAC and its supporters struggled to implement the preschool program, Houston public schools generally underserved the Mexican American community. Despite the best efforts of John J. Ruiz and others, as of 1958 the HISD had only twenty-three teachers with Spanish surnames and no systematic effort in place to hire more.

In 1958, most teachers lived in (predominantly Anglo) southwest Houston and were by and large unacquainted with the culture and specific difficulties faced by Mexican American students. Those teachers assigned to *barrio* schools were new and inexperienced, and they requested transfers as soon as they gained the necessary seniority.

In HISD during the 1950s, low attendance among Mexican American students and a high dropout rate persisted. Catholic and other parochial schools that enrolled Mexican American students usually did much better since they attempted to hire bilingual teachers and seemed more sensitive to Latin American culture. Altogether, Houston public schools had yet to address effectively the problems of education for Mexican American children.

The city still maintained its traditional ambivalence toward people of Mexican descent. Many Houstonians acknowledged that a large segment of their Mexican population was industrious and contributed to the city's progress, and Anglos of goodwill often assisted the Latin Americans' effort for advancement. Others entirely ignored the Mexican American presence or chose to emphasize the incidents of crime committed by young people with Spanish surnames. Attitudes prevailed that claimed that Mexicans, by nature, were prone to violence and "carried knives"—a traditional Anglo stereotype that saw wide usage in Houston during the 1950s.

Edna Ferber's monumental novel *Giant* (published in 1952) and the subsequent motion picture (1956), which did much to expose Texas's second-class treatment of its citizens of Mexican descent, implicated Houston in this behavior. One of the most dramatic moments in *Giant* occurred when a beauty parlor in a hotel, supposedly a thinly disguised version of Houston's historic Shamrock Hotel, refused to give service to the character Juana Benedict, a Mexican American. People commonly understood in those years that the "better" barbershops and beauty salons in Houston would not serve Mexican American customers.

In December 1958, an eleven-part series of articles by journalist Marie Dauplaise of the *Houston Chronicle* did much to bring the condition of the city's Latin Americans to wide attention. Her articles not only represented Houston's official "discovery" of its Mexican American population in the 1950s but brought readers up to date on the problems and progress of the immediate postwar period.

Flatly stated, by 1958, in spite of the best efforts of its leadership, its Anglo sympathizers, and the gains made by the expanding middle class, Houston's Latin American community faced frustrating difficulties. By that year, conservative estimates placed the city's Mexican populace at over fifty thousand. Despite its numbers, the community comprised only 5 percent of Houston's total population of one million. Still a disadvantaged group, Mexican Americans had to struggle within this urban colossus.

Dauplaise informed her readers that in every field of activity, Mexicans in Houston experienced subtle as well as overt forms of racism at the hands of mainstream society. As perhaps the most damaging example, prejudice still existed in the hiring place, although the discrimination proved hard to pinpoint. Mostly, the difficulty they faced could be found in the attitudes of the people doing the hiring. While the "No Mexicans Hired Here" signs of the 1930s had vanished, employment agents still admitted that people of Mexican descent had a tough time finding positions in the large corporations that offered the best jobs.

Although some exceptions existed, 95 percent of the "good" companies exercised the unwritten policy of not hiring Mexican Americans. People with dark complexions and a Spanish accent could expect to find it especially difficult to obtain a good job. Lighter-complexioned persons found it expedient to anglicize their names in an attempt to avoid being labeled as Latin. Mexican Americans in general could find white-collar employment mainly in retail stories, finance companies, or import-export firms. But even there they could expect to earn less than Anglos doing the same work.

As of 1958, Latin Americans in Houston could buy homes in many Anglo neighborhoods where they would once have been refused, and no evidence existed of a systematic segregation policy against Latins as there was against blacks. But real-estate agents remained reluctant to sell homes to Mexican Americans in the "better" subdivisions in the southwest and north sides of town.

Dauplaise's assessment pivoted on the biting indictment that "to a very large degree we are afflicted in Houston with Hitler's ideas of racism" in the Anglo view and treatment of Mexican Americans. This traditionally white Texan anti-Mexican sentiment in the Bayou City represented a lingering, bitter legacy from the nineteenth century. Dauplaise pointed out what the city's Latin American residents already knew. In spite of the advances made in the dozen or so years since the war, the Mexican Americans of Houston needed to go much further.

Houston Mexican Americans in all the various organizations and walks of life began to sense that only through political involvement could more substantial gains come. Their stymied expectations gave rise to increased political activism as the 1960s commenced. Even by 1958, many Latin Americans listened to the voice of protest in the person of Henry B. González, then a state senator from San Antonio, who as a gubernatorial candidate advocated across Texas for a more direct approach.

In many ways the postwar years had put Houston's Mexican American community in a position to capitalize on the more open climate of the 1960s. Their numerical growth between 1946 and 1958, their expanding middle class, and their broadened horizons as a people—along with their frustrated ambitions—would propel them into a period of unprecedented political activity.

"A Giant Awakening (No Longer the Sleeping Giant)" by Houstonian and political cartoonist Alfonso Vázquez, 1964, captured the political optimism of Mexican Americans during the 1960s. Courtesy of the Houston Metropolitan Research Center, Houston Public Library, Alfonso Vázquez Collection.

CHAPTER SEVEN

From Latin American to Chicano, 1958–1978

BETWEEN 1958 AND 1978, Houston's Mexican American community experienced a level of political activism and social ferment unprecedented in its history, a parallel to events across Texas and the Southwest. Mexican American activism in the Bayou City was in part given impetus by the black civil rights movement, but it had a life and momentum of its own.

Impelled by longstanding grievances and newfound possibilities, Houston activists formed groups to support progressive political candidates. During the 1960s, most folks in Houston discarded the term "Latin American" for "Mexican American" or "Chicano," the more militant term for *la raza,* and Houston had its own version of a Chicano protest movement operating through an array of *barrio* organizations.

Mexican Americans were a vigorous and rapidly expanding segment of Houston as the city emerged as an international metropolis. By 1960, the Mexican American community numbered seventy-five thousand. The figure had doubled to one hundred fifty thousand by 1970, or roughly 12 percent of Houston's total population, and that percentage continued to rise. Such relative growth gave politicized Chicanos the opportunity to grapple with their disadvantaged status and even make an impact outside the confines of their city.

Houston Mexican Americans gained local and state offices for the first time in significant numbers. The community's middle class expanded so that, by the 1970s, Mexican Houstonians became an economic and political force reflecting their cultural and numerical impact on the nation's fifth largest city.

The expanded horizons of Houston's Latin American community took definite political shape in 1958. Until then, most political observers considered the Latin American vote in Houston negligible, being relatively small and with little unity.

In the summer of 1958, however, the Civic Action Committee (CAC) formed. The CAC evolved from the support of Roy Elizondo, Alfonso Vázquez, E. P. Leal, and Dr. Alfredo Hernández for the candidacy of state senator Henry B. González for governor of Texas. González came to speak in Houston, and his vitality inspired these individuals to rally Houston Mexican Americans in support of his campaign.

This nucleus of people enlisted the help of friends, relatives, neighbors, and key figures from various community organizations, including Mary López, Al Matta, David Ortíz, and Roy Solíz. Many of the men were veterans of World War II and Korea. A mixture of longtime Houstonians and relative newcomers to the city comprised the group.

The CAC represented a truly grassroots organization, resembling other spontaneous political groups coalescing in Mexican American communities across the Lone Star State. Its core membership consisted of twenty to thirty people and their families, who met regularly in homes and in popular restaurants. Houston's CAC broke political ground in 1958 by holding several extremely successful fundraisers for González during his energetic although unsuccessful bid for the state's highest office. These events involved husbands, wives, children, and other relatives, thus making the political process a family affair.

Responding to the alarming reality that in 1958 only one thousand two hundred Latin Americans had paid poll taxes in Houston, CAC members launched a systematic poll tax drive within the Houston Mexican community during late 1958 and early 1959. They organized a group of over thirty people led by Alfonso Rodríguez, Walter Avalos, Genaro Flores, Ruth Valdez, and Carmen López. They concentrated their effort in Magnolia Park, the North Side, and the Second Ward, in such places as theater lobbies and food markets. On Saturday nights they would mount the stage at local night clubs during the bands' intermissions to implore Mexican American audiences to pay their poll tax so that they could make their political will felt. They solicited at predominantly Mexican American Catholic churches on Sundays.

In addition to advocating direct political participation of Latin Americans, early in 1960 the CAC joined with LULAC and the American GI Forum to study and promote a free lunch program in the Houston Independent School District. A school board member had sparked their action by remarking that Mexican American children did not need free lunches because they would rather eat "pinto beans."

In 1960, the CAC became absorbed in the presidential campaign of John F. Kennedy. Enthusiasm for the candidacy of the charismatic, progressive, Catholic senator was overwhelming among Mexican Texans. State-level

Albert Peña of San Antonio (*left*) congratulates members of Houston's Civic Action Committee (CAC) at a Viva Kennedy-Johnson victory dinner at the Santa Anita Restaurant, January 1961. Photo by commercial photographer and CAC member Alfonso Vázquez, who chronicled some of the most important events of these politically charged times. Courtesy of the Houston Metropolitan Research Center, Houston Public Library, Alfonso Vázquez Collection.

officials of the Viva Kennedy-Johnson Clubs in Texas contacted the CAC leadership to head a local effort in Houston because of the group's actions on behalf of González two years earlier. The CAC responded by establishing an office in the Second Ward, and the Viva Kennedy-Johnson Club attracted many local Mexican Americans to its ranks. The club sponsored letter-writing campaigns, poll tax drives, bumper sticker brigades, telephone banks, and community get-out-the-vote rallies in support of the entire Democratic slate. These efforts incorporated both longtime Mexican American political activists and new participants in the electoral process. The local Viva Kennedy-Johnson Club had a sense of empowerment as its candidates went on to victory.

As active as Houston's Viva Kennedy Club members were, the most influential Houston resident of Hispanic descent on the outcome of the 1960 campaign proved to be Reverend Herbert Meza, associate pastor of the Bellaire Presbyterian Church, who invited candidate Kennedy to speak to the Greater Houston Ministerial Association. At that meeting, which took place in September 1960 at the Rice Hotel, Kennedy successfully addressed his Catholicism as an issue in his quest for the White House. Until that time, many people of other faiths held serious reservations about Kennedy because of his religion, and no Roman Catholic had ever been elected president of the United States.

Herbert Meza had an interesting background. He hailed originally from Florida. His father's family had emigrated from Spain, and his mother had come directly from Cuba. The couple met, married, and lived in Ybor City, a neighborhood of Tampa where many people from Spain and Cuba had settled during the nineteenth century. Herbert was born there in 1922. His father died when Herbert was only ten years old, and his mother raised him and his elder brother as a single parent within Ybor City's vibrant Latino community. Speaking Spanish at home, young Meza naturally developed a strong sense of his Hispanic heritage. He attended Davidson College, a progressive Presbyterian institution where he honed principles he had learned from family and friends that stressed the oneness of humanity. After his ordination as a minister from Union Theological Seminary in Richmond, Virginia, Meza eventually went to Houston in 1957 to minister to working people. A Democrat, he soon became associate pastor of the Bellaire church, a more prestigious institution but in a stronghold of the Republican Party in the Houston region.

Reverend Meza also was elected vice president/program chairman of the Houston Ministerial Association in 1960 and sought to revive the organization. He invited Kennedy to speak, however, as much from his sense of fairness that a candidate for office be "judged by his ability" rather than by his religion. In particular, as Reverend Meza told this writer many years later, his Hispanic heritage largely guided this decision. Noting that "Latins have a tremendous sense of humanity," he stated that "Don Quixote is in my blood." In other words, as he put it, "a sense of the solidarity of humankind" always stood behind his actions. Reverend Meza's invitation to Kennedy to speak for himself served as perhaps the most public example of this sentiment.

As the historical record shows, John F. Kennedy appeared on September 12, 1960, spoke to the Houston audience of four hundred ministers and out-of-towners in the Crystal Ballroom of the Rice Hotel, and laid the issue of his religion to rest as a dominant campaign problem. The event appeared on national television. Meza introduced the candidate and firmly but fairly moderated the question-and-answer period, cutting short those persons who stood up simply to make hostile statements and facilitating those persons who posed direct questions. For Meza the event proved extremely tense, with some antagonistic ministers in the crowd and bright camera lights beaming down. He recalled that the candidate also seemed nervous before he spoke but once at the podium gave an effective presentation and answered the subsequent questions with aplomb. To Meza's amazement, Kennedy received a standing ovation, except for the few diehards who had long since drawn their own conclusions. Kennedy went on to be elected president, and a Houston minister of Hispanic heritage had played a pivotal role in the course of the campaign. In his classic *The Making of the President, 1960,* Theodore H. White acknowledges Reverend Meza's contribution at that meeting and credits the Houston event as the turning point in the race to victory.

In the meantime, the momentum of the successful 1960 campaign morphed the CAC into the Harris County chapter of the Political Association of Spanish-Speaking Organizations (PASO) in October 1961, with Genaro Flores and John Castillo as chairman and vice-chairman, respectively. Roy Elizondo became district chairman of PASO and eventually state chairman. Harris County PASO expanded its membership among the middle and working classes and held political functions of up to one thousand people. PASO members saw themselves as among the political vanguard of Texas Mexicans, a statewide population of two million people representing a "sleeping giant" of enormous political potential. Throughout the early and mid-1960s, they advertised on KLVL Radio Morales for Mexican Americans to vote and launched ever more ambitious voter registration drives.

Within this context of political exuberance, John F. Kennedy came back to Houston in 1963 and touched its local Hispanic residents as memorably as he had in 1960. During that fateful November trip, which culminated in his assassination in Dallas, the president landed at Houston's Hobby International Airport, where Reverend Herbert Meza was on hand once again, this time in the receiving line where Kennedy introduced him to the First Lady and briefly reminisced about their 1960 televised event together. Of broader significance, Kennedy made a historic appearance at a LULAC function at the Rice Hotel later that day—on November 21, 1963, the night before his death. President and Mrs. Kennedy and their party were in Houston to attend a banquet honoring Congressman Albert Thomas at the Sam Houston Coliseum.

Houston LULACs, under the direction of Democratic stalwart John J. Herrera, simultaneously hosted a State Director's Ball in the Grand Ballroom of the Rice Hotel, which numerous LULAC and Viva Kennedy-Johnson Club members from the 1960 campaign attended. The Kennedys and Vice President and Mrs. Lyndon Johnson stayed at the Rice Hotel and had arranged to stop by the LULAC function.

During his seventeen-minute appearance at the banquet, the president spoke to the audience about the Alliance for Progress, his administration's efforts for better relations with Latin America, as well as the good work done by LULAC in the fields of education and civic improvement. Though some Texas Hispanics had criticized Kennedy's lack of Spanish-surnamed

A night to remember. President John F. Kennedy, Vice President Lyndon B. Johnson, and party greeting Houston LULACs at the Chrystal Ballroom of the Rice Hotel, November 21, 1963, the evening before Kennedy's assassination. Kennedy is shown shaking hands with LULAC member David Adame and would be introduced to the audience by John J. Herrera. Photo courtesy of the Houston Metropolitan Research Center, Houston Public Library, Alex Arroyos Collection.

appointments, this presidential visit underscored the strong support given to Kennedy, Johnson, and the progressive wing of the Democratic Party by Houston Mexican Americans. The event also charged those in attendance with political excitement that would carry many of them through the 1960s and early 1970s. That they had visited with Kennedy during the last evening of his life gave special meaning to the support they extended him.

Meanwhile, Harris County PASO maintained its high profile in the community. In 1963, students at the University of Houston started a campus PASO group. Citywide PASO stalwarts under the successive chairmanships of Samuel S. Calderón and Manuel Crespo endorsed political candidates whom the group felt had the best interests of the Mexican American community at heart. The organization blanketed Mexican American precincts at election time with card pushers, billboards, posters, and loudspeaker trucks. During the mid-1960s, PASO allied itself successfully with other organizations in Houston, including the Harris County AFL-CIO, the Harris County Council of Organizations, the Teamsters, and the Harris County Democrats, to become the "fifth leg" in a politically influential coalition.

In addition to these local efforts, Harris County PASO became involved in the Texas Minimum Wage March of 1966, a dramatic 491-mile march to Austin by the Rio Grande Valley farmworkers from Starr County. The march grew out of a protest that began on June 1, 1966, when the United Farm Workers Association (UFWA) in Rio Grande City staged a *huelga* (strike) against local agri-business. Their demands included a $1.25 per hour wage and grower recognition of the UFWA as the farm workers' representative for collective bargaining. Labor unions and Mexican American groups in Houston immediately took up the cause. Initially, two Roman Catholic priests in Houston, Fathers Antonio González and Lawrence Peguero, collected clothing and food from their parishioners for the needy families of the strikers.

La Marcha (the march) commenced on the Fourth of July. Forty Harris County PASO members drove to Rio Grande City and participated on the first day, while others helped coordinate the action. As things progressed, Father González, whose parents had been migrant workers, and Reverend James L. Novarro, pastor of the Kashmere Baptist Temple in Houston, emerged as co-leaders of the march, supplementing the role played by union organizer Eugene Nelson. Other Houstonians participating in the march included Alfred J. Hernández, LULAC national president and a municipal judge, who joined the marchers to demonstrate his personal

The Minimum Wage March of 1966. Houston urban PASO members arrive by bus in the Valley to assist the farm workers' struggle. Photographer Alfonso Vázquez captures the enthusiasm behind these efforts. Courtesy of the Houston Metropolitan Research Center, Houston Public Library, Alfonso Vázquez Collection.

commitment to the cause; prominent LULAC and PASO supporter Tony Alvarez; and editor Moses M. Sánchez, who covered its daily events in his fledgling Houston newspaper, *El Sol*.

The march to Austin received enthusiastic support from the Texas Mexican community and other progressives. It received national media coverage and brought the deplorable conditions suffered by many rural Texas Mexicans to the attention of the country. Well organized and peaceful, the march made an impressive sight on the state capitol grounds in Austin on Labor Day, September 5, 1966. Approximately ten thousand people gathered at the capitol to celebrate this historic march for justice and dignity for Mexican Americans. *La Marcha* may well be seen as the opening salvo of the Chicano Movement in Texas.

One of the Houstonians taking an active role in the march was Lauro Cruz, who that year achieved a breakthrough in Harris County political history. In November 1966, he was elected to the Texas State Legislature, the first Mexican American from Harris County to hold state-level office, accomplishing something that John J. Herrera had first attempted almost twenty years before. Cruz was a Korean War veteran, had attended the University of Houston on the GI Bill, and had been active for many years in Houston Democratic Party politics as well as in such local organizations as the American GI Forum, LULAC, and the Lions Club.

During his campaign for the Twenty-Third District, Position Five seat, Cruz received support from a number of local Mexican American organizations, including PASO and LULAC, and he handily defeated his non-Hispanic opponents (four in the primary and one in the general election).

Cruz served for three terms and maintained high visibility in the community due to his efforts on behalf of Mexican Americans. During his tenure in office, he fostered numerous progressive causes. Springing from his involvement in the Minimum Wage March, he tried valiantly, although unsuccessfully, to put through a bill for a $1.25 per hour minimum wage in Texas. On the local level, he clashed with Mayor Louie Welch over Welch's promotion of a city sales tax. Cruz's reputation with both the Mexican American and Anglo communities as a thoughtful political realist allowed him to run a strong, though unsuccessful, race for State Treasurer in 1972.

In 1966, Felix Salazar, another veteran of the Viva Kennedy-Johnson campaign, narrowly missed winning his bid for state representative in the Democratic Party primary. Salazar, born and raised in Magnolia Park, was a member of LULAC who had worked closely with John Herrera and Felix Tijerina. An attorney by profession, Salazar had served as an assistant probate judge and would, by the mid-1970s, begin a career in the higher courts. Another distinguished Houston Mexican American jurist,

A. D. Azios, also commenced his public career in the mid-1960s, serving as Municipal Court judge from 1964 to 1972.

Other Mexican American Democrats elected as precinct judges by the mid-1960s were Ted García, Roy Solíz, George Hernández, Juanita Vera, A. John Castillo, Olga Gallegos, Frank Partida, Raul Ramírez, and Martha Díaz—all from those precincts where Mexican American voting strength mobilized for victory. Most of these individuals were strong PASO backers, had deep roots in the Houston community, and had helped to establish the Mexican American presence in the political arena.

The community quickly gave its allegiance to Lyndon B. Johnson after he assumed the presidency. In 1964, Houstonians established Viva Johnson-Humphrey Clubs and operated them in a manner similar to the Viva Kennedy-Johnson clubs of 1960. Harris County PASO remained active throughout the decade and again did its part in the Viva Humphrey-Muskie clubs in 1968, when the liberal ticket went down in defeat and broke the momentum begun in 1960. PASO evolved in the next decade and continued to produce Mexican American leaders, including Leonel J. Castillo and Ben T. Reyes, who would come to play significant roles in the affairs of Houston.

Houston PASO members Ted García (*left*) and David Ortíz (*right*) with young campaign workers during the 1964 presidential race. A PASO stalwart, photographer Alfonso Vázquez poignantly captured the family involvement by Mexican Americans in such political activities. Photo courtesy of the Houston Metropolitan Research Center, Houston Public Library, Alfonso Vázquez Collection.

During the 1960s, the Republican Party likewise began to court Mexican American voters in Houston. In some state-level elections, even PASO endorsed a few Republican candidates who opposed traditionally conservative Democrats. In the 1968 presidential campaign, an active Houston chapter of GLAD (Good Latin American Democrats for Nixon) consisted mainly of those disgruntled with what they perceived as the Democratic Party's neglect of Mexican American concerns. In 1969, a more sustained effort to curry Mexican American support for the GOP came with the founding of MARCH (Mexican American Republican Club of Houston) by some local residents.

During the years of Johnson's Great Society, its federal anti-poverty programs drew the interest of Houston's Mexican American activists. Such efforts seemed long overdue and desperately needed in the *barrios*. Chief among the local responses to the availability of grants and other money was the implementation of an employment program by LULAC Council 60. Houston LULACs began discussing the idea of a job-placement referral program in the spring of 1964. They convinced the national organization to endorse the project in February 1965, and Houston became the pilot city for the program. In April 1965, LULAC Council 60, using volunteer staffing, opened the first "Jobs for Progress" placement office. Subsequently, Corpus Christi LULACs began a similar office.

In June 1966, the federal government funded the concept (titled Operation SER/Jobs for Progress, Inc.) as a joint project between LULAC and the American GI Forum. Operation SER (named after the Spanish verb "to be") provided remedial education opportunities as well as job training and placement for Mexican Americans across the Southwest.

The untiring efforts of Houstonians in Operation SER's development reflected their desire to advance the cause of Mexican Americans during these reform-minded years. By the early 1970s, the program, which had largely germinated in Houston, assisted thousands of Mexican Americans across the nation. In its advocacy of this project and others, Council 60 also produced another LULAC national president, Alfred J. Hernández, during these years. As president, Hernández became part of a triumvirate (which included John Herrera and Felix Tijerina from the 1950s), who made Houston a focal point of that important organization.

During the 1960s, LULAC Councils 60 and 22 no longer remained the only representatives of that group active in Houston. Younger Mexican Americans began to establish new councils—by the mid-1970s, over a half dozen operated in the Bayou City. The new councils often advocated change more vigorously than the original two.

In 1970, Felix Fraga became director of Ripley House, one of Houston's leading *barrio* social service agencies. Photo courtesy of the Houston Metropolitan Research Center, Houston Public Library, Houston Press Collection.

Local governmental efforts, such as the Houston City Job Fair, initiated by the Welch administration in 1967, targeted Mexican American neighborhoods. This program involved *barrio* volunteers who assisted residents, particularly youth, in finding summer employment.

Mexican Americans began to assume executive positions in anti-poverty programs. John E. Castillo, a PASO stalwart, became secretary to the board of directors of the Houston/Harris County Economic Opportunity Organization in early 1967. In August 1970, William Gutiérrez became the first Mexican American to direct Wesley House, the Methodist social service agency in the North Side *barrio*. Also in 1970, Felix Fraga became Director of Ripley House in the Second Ward. A popular figure in Houston, Fraga had grown up near *El Alacrán* and had worked for Neighborhood Centers since 1946.

While the traditional groups continued their activities, more militant voices, especially among the youth, came to the fore. Adopting the term "Chicano" as a form of self-designation and ethnic solidarity, these individuals formed organizations of their own, published community newspapers as forums for their ideas, and represented another facet in the continuing quest for Mexican American identity in Houston.

The most important of these periodicals were *Compass* and *Papel Chicano. Compass* began publication in April 1967, as a newspaper of LULAC Council 406, but quickly adopted a more political posture. Its publishers, Felix and Lena Ramírez, two North Side *barrio* residents, helped to establish the nationwide Chicano Press Association. By 1969, the Association had twenty-eight newspapers through which they exchanged community information. The commencement of *Compass,* on the heels of the Minimum Wage March, in many respects marked the beginning of Houston's Chicano Movement as it coincided with the more strident activities of Houston Mexican Americans.

Papel Chicano started publishing in the summer of 1970 through the efforts of a group of younger people including Johnny Almendárez, Carlos Calbillo, Leo Tanguma, Kris Vásquez, Enrique Pérez, Al Durán, and others. From its office in Magnolia Park, *Papel Chicano* reported grassroots activism taking place in such areas as the El Dorado Subdivision, South Houston, Denver Harbor, the North Side, Magnolia Park, the Second Ward, and Manchester.

During the late 1960s and early 1970s, these militant newspapers reported on a plethora of community actions and complaints, including the generally poor city services the *barrios* received and the pervasive air pollution suffered in areas along the ship channel. They criticized the more traditional social and civic clubs of Houston for not moving fast enough in promoting Mexican American rights, often labeling them as *vendidos* ("sell-outs"). These Chicano voices ridiculed local Anglo politicians such as Mayor Welch and called the Houston Police Department under Chief Herman Short "a bigot, racist corps," a characterization of HPD with which many in the city would have agreed. The militant press protested the economic domination of the community by Anglos and decried the growing drug problem in the *barrios.*

Chicano activists in the late 1960s and early 1970s questioned the whole idea of assimilation into mainstream American society as a false hope and undesirable ideal. They posited that Chicanos were part of *la raza* and should preserve their unique cultural personality as a contribution to the pluralistic society of the United States. They saw Houston as part of *Aztlán,* the spiritual nation of the Aztecs in the southwestern United States, and felt that such ethnicity was a source of pride.

As part of this world view, Chicano activists also openly doubted that traditional education, the totem of the 1950s Latin American vision of the future, was *the* answer to their people's problems since they felt that the roots of their difficulty sprang primarily from prejudice and discrimination by Anglo society.

Houston militants responded to more than local issues. They identified with the Chicano school boycotts and other activism taking place in other parts of the state and nation. For them, the examples of Céasar Chávez of California, Reies López Tijerina of New Mexico, Rodolfo "Corky" González of Colorado, and José Angel Gutiérrez of Texas seemed especially inspirational.

In April 1968, young Houstonians under the direction of Joseph Rojo and George Rivera planned and hosted a *Raza Unida* conference. Activists from across the city participated, and the highly publicized meeting called for a "peaceful revolution" for Mexican Americans in Houston. During the summer of 1968, another group calling itself *Las Familias Unidas del Segundo Barrio* took up this cause by protesting the poor city services that plagued that area.

Two branches of the Mexican American Youth Organization (MAYO) emerged during this period as probably the most radical of these initial groups. Founded by José Angel Gutiérrez in San Antonio, Texas in 1967, MAYO spread to Houston and took root both in the *barrios* and on the University of Houston campus.

The MAYO chapter at the University of Houston evolved from a late 1960s group called the League of Mexican Americans Students (LOMAS). LOMAS had taken shape under Tatcho Mindiola Jr., Ramón Villagómez, Al Pérez, Ninfa Zepeda, George Rangel, Susie Quintanilla, and others. They were active across a spectrum of campus affairs, seeking to make the University community aware of Mexican American issues. In March 1969, for example, LOMAS hosted speaker Rodolfo "Corky" González of the Denver-based Crusade for Justice. As students during the most intense period of social ferment, these young thinkers sought to formulate an intellectual framework for *Chicanismo*—what it meant to be Mexican American. By the end of the decade, the members of LOMAS transformed their group into a MAYO chapter.

In 1971, Campus MAYO, under the leadership of Elliot Navarro, saw one of its members, María Jiménez, a Magnolia Park resident, elected vice president of the University of Houston student body, the first Mexican American ever to achieve such a position in the school's student government. As events unfolded over the next thirty years, Jiménez would emerge as one of the more honorable, committed activists in Houston.

Such activity by Chicano students helped lay the groundwork by 1974 for the establishment of a Mexican American Studies Program at the

University of Houston. Founded by MAYO members and initially administered by educator Guadalupe Quintanilla, it later expanded under the direction of Tatcho Mindiola Jr., who had joined the Department of Sociology after finishing graduate work at Brown University. Nor was such campus activity limited to the University of Houston. By 1970, sixty Chicano students at San Jacinto College in Pasadena formed MASS, the Mexican American Student Association.

Houston's Community MAYO, as it was known, may have been the most vociferous of the militant groups. Like Campus MAYO, it took shape in the late 1960s through the efforts of Carlos Calbillo, Benito Maldonado, Raúl Gutiérrez, Daniel Reséndez, Sarah Baéz, Andy Vázquez, and others. With a membership of several dozen young people, it involved itself in numerous actions that attracted a great deal of media coverage.

Community MAYO reached perhaps its most active period in 1970, when it spearheaded a series of events. By that time its ranks included Yolanda Garza Birdwell, Walter Birdwell, Gregory Salazar, Poncho Ruíz, and several other militants who personified the organization's politicized posture. In February 1970, for example, its members led a coalition of representatives of several groups that occupied a vacant Presbyterian Church in the North Side and tried to turn it into a Chicano community center. They were evicted, but along with members of the Campus MAYO chapter, the activists countered with a seventy-five-person protest at Houston's First Presbyterian Church. Ultimately, the North Side church became the predominantly Mexican American Juan Marcos Presbyterian Church.

On the heels of this action, a highly visible (and rowdy) demonstration took place by MAYO members at the April 21 ceremonies at the San Jacinto Battleground. This protest illustrated the younger Chicanos' desire to confront the Anglo-Texan's ethnocentric view of history that had shaped attitudes toward people of Mexican descent. It demonstrated the militants' opposite view from that of the LULACs, who in the 1940s and 1950s had embraced the historic role of *Tejanos* in the battle.

MAYO activists likewise pushed, within the *Comité Moratorio Chicano*, to hold a July 26, 1970 Chicano moratorium and anti-war march from Hidalgo Park in Magnolia Park involving over one thousand people. The streets of Magnolia Park reverberated with cries of *"Raza sí—Guerra no."* The realization among Houston Chicanos in the late 1960s that Mexican Americans, like other minority groups, served in high percentages in the Vietnam War spurred one of the most crucial flashpoints of discontent. Chicano casualities were higher than other groups. The local press carried photo after photo of young Houston Mexican American soldiers, sailors, and Marines killed or wounded in action, reminiscent of the community's experiences with World War II and Korea.

MAYO members supported the activities of other Houston Mexican American groups as they took action against the myriad of annoyances they faced in everyday life. In 1970, East Side residents, along with a MAYO contingent, protested the lack of adequate facilities at Eastwood and Settegast Parks. In July of that year, a group of over seventy residents, most from the Mexican American middle class, were arrested for protesting the operation of the stench-ridden North Loop landfill.

Members of Houston MAYO participated in protests held in the South Texas town of Mathis over the death of Dr. Fred Logan Jr. in the summer of 1970. In mid-July, a San Patricio County deputy sheriff had fatally shot Dr. Logan amid suspicious circumstances after arresting him. Logan had operated a clinic for Mexican Americans in Mathis and had been a voice for the local poor Chicanos, and many—including his family—felt that his killing had political motives. MAYO members and other community people viewed Logan as an Anglo martyr to the cause of *la raza*. Many of these participants saw the Logan affair as a watershed in the mobilization of Chicano activists from across the state.

In the fall of 1970, a deluge of protest calls occurred over the use of the "Frito Bandito" character in local television commercials. Many Mexican Americans around the nation saw this animated cartoon figure as a negative image. Houston Mexican American groups met with local television management to sensitize it to Chicano concerns. During the 1970s, Houston Chicanos systematically pressured media to hire Mexican Americans.

Militant Chicano voices helped raise the cry in the early 1970s against the ever-present police brutality in Houston. *Papel Chicano* cited examples of alleged beatings and other violations of Mexican Americans' civil rights, as well as harassment of Chicano activists by police officers who habitually displayed disrespectful and threatening behavior toward people of all colors. During these times, community leaders often advised their constituents simply to avoid the HPD rather than receive abuse at the hands of this law enforcement agency.

Houston's Community MAYO received most attention, however, for its participation in an altercation at a meeting of the Houston Independent School District Board of Trustees. The longstanding difficulties that Mexican Americans had experienced in the school system came to a head by the fall of 1970. MAYO helped to bring national media attention to these problems in education when, at the conclusion of the regularly scheduled

Members of Houston's community Mexican American Youth Organization (MAYO) struggle with Houston Independent School District officials in the altercation at the school board meeting, September 14, 1970. Photo courtesy of the *Houston Chronicle*.

meeting on the evening of September 14, members of the group insisted that they be allowed to present a list of grievances relative to *barrio* students. A general "riot" occurred, and police arrested a number of young Chicanos.

The confrontation between the HISD Board of Trustees and MAYO came at the beginning of the Mexican American boycott of the Houston schools, perhaps the most significant action of the Chicano Movement in the city. As early as 1968, echoing complaints of several Mexican American interest groups around town, the Chicano press noted that "Houston schools are ripe for an internal revolution" as parents became militant about the continuing poor educational atmosphere. Not only did Chicanos complain about inadequate facilities, teacher abuse, and insensitive administrators, but by 1969, they were upset because HISD had not fully implemented a federal free lunch program for deprived children after it had been adopted locally the previous year.

The school boycott came, however, in the fall of 1970, after the U.S. Fifth Circuit Court of Appeals, in *Ross* v. *Eckels,* on August 25, 1970, had directed HISD to carry out a desegregation plan that unduly affected Chicano children. The court's plan paired white and black students and exchanged them through bussing for racial integration. The plan included only twenty-five elementary schools, less than 10 percent of all schools in HISD. These twenty-five were primarily in northeast Houston and involved mainly Mexican Americans as the "whites" in the process.

The Mexican American community immediately protested being asked to bear the brunt of desegregation. Although the court had picked the schools to be paired, concerned Mexican Americans suspected that Anglo-Houstonians had played a hand in the selection of Mexican Americans to shoulder the burden of pairing. For them, it seemed to be another case of the establishment forcing blacks and Chicanos to vie with one another for a position in society, artificially pitting two deprived groups against one another.

After HISD officials refused to recognize Mexican Americans as an identifiable ethnic minority and hesitated to correct the imbalance in the pairing plan, a group calling itself the Mexican American Education Council (MAEC), under the leadership of Leonel Castillo and Abraham Ramírez Jr., called for a Chicano boycott of the schools when classes began on August 31.

Some three thousand five hundred of the approximately six thousand Mexican American students impacted by the court-ordered plan stayed home in an initial three-week-long strike, and many attended "*Huelga* Enrichment Centers" at various churches around town and taught by volunteer teachers. To underscore the seriousness of the situation, in September, the first rally of more than five thousand Mexican Houstonians who began the boycott took place in Eastwood Park. MAEC urged all thirty-six thousand six hundred Mexican American students in HISD to boycott the schools until the district declared that Mexican Americans comprised an identifiable ethnic minority.

MAEC consisted of Houston groups sensitive to the educational needs of *la raza;* each group had three representatives on MAEC's general assembly. MAEC became the voice of the community in the Bayou City seeking change and equity within HISD. Although negotiations between MAEC and school district officials brought an end to the boycott and enrichment centers in three weeks, the tense situation erupted again in January 1971, when HISD presented a modified pairing plan that the community still found objectionable.

MAEC called for a renewal of the school strike and instituted *huelga* schools in February. Various schools of this type functioned for several years. The first of these *huelga* schools opened at Juan Marcos Church with Cammy Reyes as its principal. Concerned parents continued to picket HISD headquarters as MAEC attorneys filed a motion to intervene in the school case. The *huelgistas* and their supporters became outraged when a

Principal José I. Torres and students of the Juan Marcos *huelga* school, 3600 Fulton Street, in Houston's North Side *barrio*, ca. 1971. Photo by Ed Gaida. Courtesy of the Houston Metropolitan Research Center, Houston Public Library.

federal judge ruled against MAEC in May, stating, "Content to be 'White' for these many years, now, when the shoe begins to pinch, the would-be interveners wish to be treated not as whites but as an 'identifiable minority group.'" They viewed this ruling as insensitive to a century of abuse suffered by Mexican Americans in Texas schools. Certainly the decision did not reflect an understanding of the historic problems Mexican Americans had with ethnic labeling.

Scholar Margarita Melville notes that the U.S. Supreme Court ultimately terminated Houston's pairing issue in June 1973 by ruling, in a similar school case out of Denver, that mixing blacks with Chicanos did not constitute a valid method of desegregation. By then, however, most of the striking Chicano students had long since returned to HISD classrooms.

Clearly, the Houston Mexican American community gained from the boycott and *huelga* schools. This action prompted the city to address further the problems of Mexican American education. The school district began to recognize Mexican Americans as an identifiable ethnic minority in its planning and hired additional Chicano teachers. By 1972, HISD reportedly had 300 Mexican American teachers, a startling turnaround from previous decades and a sign of good intentions. The episode also demonstrated that the Mexican American community could speak in a unified manner and get results, and the struggle invigorated many young Chicano educators to work for the concerns of *barrio* students. In his study of this period, author Guadalupe San Miguel Jr. aptly concludes that Mexican Americans "became militant and 'brown'"—rather than claiming to be "white" as in previous decades—"in their quest for educational justice."

By the summer of 1972, Mexican American teachers in HISD, under the chairmanship of Luis Cano, a Chicano studies instructor, had organized the Hispanic Teachers Caucus within the Houston Teachers Association. Cano had been instrumental, along with Yolanda Navarro, Roland Laurenzo, and Froilán Hernández, in the founding of the Association for the Advancement of Mexican Americans (AAMA) during the summer of 1970. Under Cano's leadership and almost herculean efforts in 1973, AAMA developed the George I. Sánchez High School, an alternative school for dropouts and other Mexican American youths who had difficulty in the pubic educational system. Despite chronic underfunding, a feature of *barrio* institutions, AAMA achieved remarkable successes with these young people.

In the midst of the school boycott, Leonel Castillo and MAEC began planning a Chicano university. This institution, begun in 1970 as the Hispanic International University (HIU), was based on the university-without-walls concept. Its courses initially targeted the bilingual and bicultural student. It eventually became Houston International University.

During these efforts for Chicano educational advancement, Houston lost the most illustrious public educator that its Mexican American community had ever produced when Armand Yramategui died at the hands of robbers on January 27, 1970. Born in the Bayou City in 1923 and christened Manuel Armando Yramategui, this remarkable individual was the son of 1920s Mexican immigrants Casimiro Yramategui and María Encarnacion Pérez García de Yramategui. Casimiro held a good job with the Southern Pacific Railroad yards as a machinist near where he purchased a home on McKee Street in the near North Side. Casimiro had also fostered education and intellectual exploration in Armando and his younger brother Hector. After serving in World War II, Armando graduated from Rice Institute in 1947 with a major in electrical engineering.

Yramategui found his real passion in life, however, when he was struck by the wonders of nature. During the early 1950s, working as a real-estate developer of wooded property, Armand Yramategui became enthralled with the trees along Buffalo Bayou and became involved in bird watching with the local Outdoor Nature Club. Savoring the beauty of wild habitats, he developed as one of the state's outstanding naturalists. He won election as president of the Texas Ornithological Society and ultimately head of the Texas Conservation Council. He also taught science for a time in local public schools and became a self-taught astronomer.

His knowledge led him to become curator of the Burke Baker Planetarium in 1964. In that position, he soon appeared on local television public service spots three mornings per week to explain the wonders of the night sky to children, a role that endeared him to thousands of Houstonians. The children learned from him about the early astronomers, what constellations could be seen, and their links to Greek and other mythologies. He often spoke to school classes about these topics, always taking time to talk with youngsters regarding such matters.

Reflective by nature, Yramategui told a newspaper reporter in 1969 that he saw the space program as "a reflection of what the Creator has endowed man with—an infinite intellect for increasing man's understanding" that "will bring man eventually to a Utopia." People often asked him about his last name, to which he would explain that Yramategui originated from the Basque region of northern Spain and that poetically it meant "one who draws inspiration from the view from the top of a mountain."

As he emerged as a leading force in Texas nature conservation efforts during the 1950s, Armand Yramategui had many disciples among Houston's upper-middle-class environmentalists who looked to him for inspiration. U.S. congressman Bob Eckhardt saw Yramategui as the citizen most responsible for enacting the Texas Open Beaches Act because of a successful signature campaign Yramategui spearheaded in 1959 for that legislation to overcome special interests standing in the way. In the 1960s, Armand Yramategui was a household name in many circles.

On the evening of January 27, 1970, Yramategui traveled down the Southwest Freeway to escape the bright lights of the city so that he could photograph the Tago-Sato-Kosaka comet, a celestial body that he had done much to popularize among Houstonians. Unfortunately, he had a flat tire. Three individuals who randomly came along at first offered to assist him but decided to rob him and, in the course of this felony, mindlessly shot him to death by the side of the highway. The passing of Armand Yramategui deprived the nation of a deeply sensitive, gentle, philosophical, and productive human being.

Yramategui's associates carried on his work, however, when they successfully pushed for a measure he had championed to save Middle Bayou near Pasadena as a natural habitat. These efforts resulted in the changing of the waterway's name to Armand Bayou and creation of the Armand

Bayou Nature Center in the 1970s, which eventually consisted of approximately two thousand five hundred acres of pristine bayou lands being set aside. It amounted to a tribute to a renowned environmentalist who had begun life as a child of unassuming Mexican immigrants.

Bilingual education in Houston, another important issue in the schools, was upgraded around this time. Chicano activists called for more relevance in education for their community and especially advocated federal support of bilingual education in Houston after such legislation passed in the U.S. Congress in 1967. HISD had commenced its bilingual program in 1959 under educator Raúl Muñoz. It had expanded on the elementary school level in the 1960s through local funding and under federal entitlements programs. In 1974, under state mandate, HISD began systematically installing bilingual education in the lower grades. As of the 1974–75 school year, HISD boasted thirty-one bilingual teachers and thirty-five aides in the elementary and secondary schools. Thereafter, rapid expansion of the program was the order of the day.

Chicano activist educators realized that while education did not necessarily provide the key to happiness or "success," it remained essential in their world view because it gave individuals the ability to express themselves within and for their community. These educators tried not only to make existing institutions more sensitive to Mexican American concerns but also to build alternative programs of more relevance to the lives of their people.

As the boycott and *huelga* schools flourished, other actions continued across the spectrum of Mexican American affairs. Beginning in the late 1960s, Houston Chicano activists initiated boycotts of local stores selling grapes and other produce from companies involved in labor disputes with Céasar Chávez's United Farm Workers. By 1970, younger activists like Daniel Bustamante and Eddie Canales advocated *la causa* (the cause) of the Texas farmworkers in the Bayou City.

By 1971, a Houston branch of the Brown Berets, a militant organization comprised mainly of young men from the North Side, formed. Concerned with the drug problem among youth, members patrolled parks and back alleys to prevent drug use. They especially watched for inhalant abuse, which was a major issue in the community. The Brown Berets also assisted with many of the marches and community events in conjunction with other activist organizations, since some of its membership overlapped with other groups.

In the early 1970s, young Mexican American women in Houston began to express their concern over the plight of the Chicana and formed several

LA CONFERENCIA
De Mujeres
Por La Raza

UNDER THE AUSPICES OF THE

YWCA

Young Women's Christian Association

May 28 - 30, 1971
Houston, Texas

The cover of the program for *La Conferencia De Mujeres Por La Raza*, 1971, a major expression of Houston's militant Chicanas and a milestone for Mexican American women activists across Texas. Courtesy of the Houston Metropolitan Research Center, Houston Public Library, John E. Castillo Collection.

vocal women's groups. They felt that men dominated all levels of society and exploited women. Under the auspices of the Magnolia Park YWCA, several hundred women from different states met on May 28–30, 1971 at *La Conferencia de Mujeres Por la Raza*. Houston activists participating in the conference included, among others, Grace Gil Olivárez, Yolanda Garza Birdwell, María Jiménez, Gloria Guardiola, and Bertha Hernández. Symbolic of the temper of the conference, the keynote address was entitled "Machismo—What Are We Up Against?"

La Conferencia de Mujeres included lively discussions as the delegates expressed their exasperation with male domination. Many noted that middle-class Anglo approaches proved irrelevant to their lives as people who were, in the words of anthropologist Margarita Melville, "twice a minority." Unfortunately, the conference concluded with a walkout by many delegates from Houston and California who felt that the meeting had included too few *barrio* women and too many middle-class issues.

One of the most recognizable groups of Chicano activists in Houston during this period was the Houston branch of *La Raza Unida* Party, which existed as the only independent Mexican American political party in the city's history. *La Raza Unida* Party began in 1970 in Crystal City, Texas and soon found spiritual support in the Houston *barrios* because of the perceived insensitivity of both major parties to Mexican American problems.

La Raza Unida Party in Houston held its organizational meeting at Wesley House on the North Side in September 1971 and drew much of its membership from MAYO activists. There, they planned the building of the local party organization and selected officers, including Edward Castillo, a University of Houston student, and Gloria Ramírez, a community worker, to preside jointly over the assembly.

Houston's *Raza Unida* Party also held precinct conventions in the North Side and the Second Ward and hosted its first countywide convention in May 1972 to elect a body of county officers. It sent Daniel Bustamante, an early MAYO and *Raza Unida* stalwart, to the 1972 state convention held in San Antonio.

Although Houston's *Raza Unida* Party did not field a candidate in 1972, it strongly supported the statewide slate of candidates, especially

Campaign workers in Moody Park for Houston's *La Raza Unida* Party in 1972. *Standing left to right:* Dolores Rodríguez, Richard Partida, Virginia Ramírez, Charley Guerrero, Gloria Ramírez, Dolores Castillo, David Lerme, Poncho Ruíz, and José Bustamante; *Seated left to right:* Rachel Rodríguez and Mary Puente. Photo courtesy of the Houston Metropolitan Research Center, Houston Public Library, Alfonso Vázquez Collection.

Leonel J. Castillo, 1972, after his election as Houston's first Mexican American City Controller. Castillo was among the community's most admired Hispanic public officials. Photo courtesy of the *Houston Chronicle*.

gubernatorial candidate Ramsey Muñiz. A native of Corpus Christi, Muñiz generated a great deal of excitement and publicity when he campaigned in the Bayou City.

La Raza Unida in Houston reached its zenith in 1974 when it fielded several candidates for state legislative positions, including Ruben Rabazo, Victor Vega, and María Jiménez. Rabazo and Vega had both been active in LULAC, an illustration of the overlap among all Mexican American organizations despite the friction that often existed between the groups in these turbulent years. In 1974, the Houston chapter hosted the *Raza Unida* state convention. It again supported Ramsey Muñiz's unsuccessful bid for the governorship, and its candidates amazed political observers by garnering a surprising number of votes from the Mexican American electorate.

Houston's *Raza Unida* Party ran several candidates in 1976 and was on the ballot again in 1978, but by these years its activity had dwindled. Despite its lack of election wins, the party had provided Houston with an example of articulate Chicano political activism and made a lasting impact on the local scene. Its members and candidates would go on to other activities where their assertiveness provided the community with a needed boost.

During the 1970s, other, more moderate Mexican Americans began to gain political office in Houston and Harris County. Attorney David Lopez won election in 1971 to the Houston School board as part of the Citizens for Good Schools slate of candidates. Leonel Castillo was elected controller of the City of Houston that same year and was twice reelected.

Perhaps most important, Houstonians began to see candidates with Spanish surnames win races and take their place among the decision makers of the city.

Municipal court judge Armando V. Rodríguez was appointed justice of the peace for the Sixth Precinct in 1973 and was elected the following year to the first of many terms. After a brief stint as justice of the peace, in 1974 A. D. Azios was appointed judge of County Court of Law Number 3. Also in 1974, Mayor Fred Hofheinz appointed Abraham Ramírez Jr., Angel Fraga, and Rosemary Saucillo as judges of the Municipal Court, the latter being the first Mexican American woman ever to hold that position. Like his father, Mayor Hofheinz represented another of the many *amigos del pueblo* who sought to incorporate Mexican Americans into the fabric of Houston society in a meaningful way.

Raúl C. Martínez, the veteran Houston police officer, received appointment as Harris County constable of the Sixth Precinct in 1973 and won the first of his many terms in 1974. Richard C. Vara won election as Harris County justice of the peace in 1974, at the unusually young age of twenty-four.

In 1972, Ben T. Reyes began his long and influential career in public office by winning election as Texas state representative for the Eighty-Seventh District. Reyes was a young Marine Corps Vietnam War veteran who had grown up poor in Denver Harbor. A Democratic Party and PASO activist, Reyes served his district ably and advocated generally for Mexican American concerns. From these beginnings, the articulate Reyes became perhaps the dominant political figure in Houston Chicano affairs.

During the early 1970s, one of Houston's most eloquent voices, Patricio Flores, a diocesan priest and pastor of Houston's inner-city parishes of St. Joseph and St. Stephen's, received appointment as auxiliary bishop of the San Antonio Archdiocese. The son of local farm workers, Flores had experienced the pangs of hunger as a child and knew the hardships of being Mexican American. He had been influenced by such early activists as John J. Herrera and Alfred J. Hernández. As the only Mexican American bishop at that time, Flores toured the United States speaking out for the poor while winning the love of his people.

La raza in Houston continued to make its cultural presence known. In 1964, Carlos García began his long-running and popular television

A GOOD MAN
FOR A CHANGE

VOTE AGAIN FOR BEN
BEN T. REYES
STATE REPRESENTATIVE
DISTRICT 87

Campaign flyer for Ben T. Reyes, whose
election as state representative in 1972
marked the beginning of his long, influential career in public office. Photo courtesy
of the Houston Metropolitan Research
Center, Houston Public Library, John E.
Castillo Collection.

program *Cita Con Carlos* (*Date With Carlos*), a milestone for the city's Hispanics in the media. At first featuring talent from Mexico, García's program eventually adopted a bilingual format and focused on local musical artists. Al Zarzana, a local non-Hispanic who was very involved with
the Mexican American community, initiated weekend Spanish-language
programming for Houston-Galveston area television in the early 1970s.
Zarzana later operated a string of Spanish-language suburban movie the-
aters. As the decade progressed, the city's major television stations, at the
urging of Chicano groups, commenced several public service programs
directed at the Mexican American populace. *Hola Amigos* on KHOU-TV
(under producer Al Varela), KPRC-TV's *Reflejos Del Barrio* (under founding producer Tony Bruni), and *Mexican American Dialogue* (under producer Angie Pruneda) on KTRK-TV were the most important of the early
programming that brought Mexican American issues to Houston viewers.

In May 1971, Richard Pérez, a community activist, Vietnam veteran, and nephew of the noted musician Eloy Pérez, began a radio program on Radio Pacifica entitled *Chicanos Can Too*. Concurrently he spearheaded *La Junta Grande* at Jeppesen Stadium—a large gathering of Mexican American musicians, both old and young, vividly illustrating the continuity of "Tex-Mex" music and culture.

Also in May 1971, widely known Houston Chicano artist Leo Tanguma and others held a four-day *la raza* art festival at Ripley House in the Second Ward. Artists came from across the state to participate in the affair, which stressed arts and crafts for the average *barrio* resident. Tanguma headed another project that in the early 1970s created a large Chicano mural on the exterior wall of the Continental Can Company building, 5800 Canal Street. The mural exalted the historic struggles of Mexican Americans. Tanguma's project ultimately involved dozens of local Chicano artists, and the mural is considered by many to be the major expression of Chicano public art in Houston. It existed for decades without being defaced in this industrial area, testimony to the respect in which even the most reckless *barrio* youth held it.

The mural at 5800 Canal Street, entitled *The Rebirth of Our Nationality,* Houston's most important artistic statement during its Chicano Movement. The mural stretched 240 feet in length and was completed in 1972–73. Leo Tanguma served as its project director, creator, and principal artist, while other such notable local artists as Atanacio P. Davila participated in its painting. Photo by the author, 1986.

During the late 1960s, Juan Coronado initiated an annual *fiestas patrias* parade down Main Street on September 16, in many ways a revival of the earlier *Diez y Seis* celebrations. The long-term success of the *Diez y Seis* festivities was ensured, however, by the 1971 chartering of the *Fiestas Patrias* organization by Rita and Armando Rodríguez, A. John Castillo, Johnny Matta, and Rita Villanueva. Under chairwoman Dolores Gallegos Rodríguez, *Fiestas Patrias* greatly expanded this cultural event. It coexisted with *El Comité Patriótico Mexicano,* the other, more Mexican-oriented group that commemorated Mexican national holidays and had its roots in the first decade of the century. A large parade would yearly entertain Houstonians, along with the crowning of a festival queen and a week of events.

Altogether, this twenty-year period in Houston reflected the increase in numbers, strength, and activism of Mexican Americans across the Southwest. This activity had taken place within the context of a burgeoning Mexican American population. By the mid-1970s, Houston's Mexican American community could well have numbered two hundred thousand, making it second only to San Antonio in Texas. Participation by average Mexican Americans in neighborhood civic associations, advisory committees, community service agencies, and other advocacy groups stood at an all-time high. They involved themselves as never before in local, regional, and national conferences dealing with urban affairs, thus injecting the Mexican American perspective into the decision-making process.

While most Mexican Houstonians were not personally active in the overtly political groups of the movement, they did become sensitized because of the general climate of self-expression. Certainly most agreed that society needed to address the problems that the activists sought to rectify. Emblematic of these unresolved troubles were the case of Joe Campos Torres and the Moody Park riot, which occurred at the end of this period.

In the second week of May 1977 came the shocking news that Joe Campos Torres, a twenty-three-year-old resident of the city, had met his death while in the custody of Houston police officers. The facts gradually came to light that police arrested Torres in an East Side disturbance on May 6 and took him to a secluded spot on Buffalo Bayou, where he received a severe beating. When the officers took Torres to jail, the prisoner was in such poor condition that the desk sergeant would not book him. Instead of ferrying him to the hospital for care as they were instructed to do, the officers took him back to the Bayou and administered another beating. At that point, Torres was allegedly pushed into the Bayou, where he drowned.

A tour boat captain discovered the body on May 8. An army veteran, Torres received full military honors at his burial in Veterans Cemetery.

The Mexican American community responded with justifiable outrage. Regardless of the strides made in so many areas, here was an example of the lingering problems. The case of Joe Campos Torres, occurring forty years after the similar Elidio Cortéz affair, provided stark evidence of the ongoing police brutality that the Chicano press had complained of so vehemently.

Mamie García, head of LULAC Eighth District, demanded an immediate investigation of the episode by the U.S. Department of Justice. State representative Ben Reyes likewise called for an outside inquiry into what he saw as a case of "rampant brutality" by the police. A series of community meetings and protests over Torres's death included all segments of the Mexican American community, and a group called *Barrios Unidos en Defensa* organized to protest the death. Everyone worked toward some sort of justice in the case. The community understood what all thinking citizens knew; that is, anyone of color or within the white counterculture still found themselves susceptible to violence at the hands of many within the HPD.

To add insult to injury, after several well-publicized trials, the half-dozen officers involved in Torres's death were convicted of lesser charges. Juries convicted two of negligent homicide and found three guilty of

Beginning of a demonstration at Moody Park, October 8, 1977, over the death of Joe Campos Torres at the hands of Houston police officers. Photo courtesy of the *Houston Chronicle*.

violating Torres's civil rights, while one officer pleaded guilty to a federal misdemeanor assault. All received relatively light jail sentences. Mexican Americans and many Houstonians of all colors felt the results represented a mockery of justice.

On the evening of May 7, 1978, almost one year after the discovery of Torres's body in Buffalo Bayou, a riot occurred in Moody Park on the city's North Side. Community leaders had counseled peaceful support of the ongoing, meaningful reforms that Chief Harry Caldwell sought to implement in the police department, but the riot exploded from the *barrio's* frustration over the Torres affair as well as with deplorable neighborhood conditions.

The riot began when some of the celebrants at the *Cinco de Mayo* festivities (being held at Moody Park) turned on park police officers who tried to intervene in a fight between two young men. The crowd of angry, alienated youths swelled to over 150 and threw rocks and beer bottles at police and passers-by. In the ensuing night of violence, the rioters set several automobiles afire and burned or looted nearby stores as the police, city officials, and Mexican American community leaders did their best to contain the trouble.

Before the long night ended, fifteen people, including two reporters and three police officers, had sustained injuries and thousands of dollars in property damage had occurred. The following night, more violence flared as police confronted rock-throwing bands of youth in the area. Police arrested several dozen persons before the mischief ended.

Like the Torres case, the Moody Park riot received much media play. Although many people blamed alcohol and a small band of outside agitators for sparking the young people to violence, all agreed that the outburst ultimately stemmed from a combination of anger over the relatively light sentences handed down to the officers involved in the death of Joe Campos Torres and the poor quality of life in parts of the immediate Moody Park area.

Many of the youths who participated in the fracas lived at Irvington Village, a run-down, predominantly Mexican American housing project of 318 units that bordered Moody Park's south side. Built in 1942, Irvington Village's dilapidated condition symbolized the many chronic problems of *barrio* life. Its young people lived in poverty, lacking adequate motivation, education, or supervision, and found their escape in drugs and alcohol. As a result of the riot, city and community leaders initiated a plan to alleviate the conditions around the project and continued to upgrade the professionalism of the Houston police.

The tumult dramatically reminded residents of the problems so many Mexican Americans still faced despite the advances of the last twenty years. Large numbers still occupied positions near the bottom rung of society and remained isolated in the *barrios*. On the other hand, Mexican Americans increasingly moved into even the most exclusive Anglo subdivisions, and intermarriage with non-Hispanics occurred commonly. In more than token numbers, Mexican Americans entered the professions and found employment with corporations and businesses that had excluded them prior to 1958. Most of the institutional barriers to Mexican American advancement had come down as a result of this twenty-year period of activism.

Across the socioeconomic spectrum, most Mexican Houstonians lived as active, bicultural participants in their city. The community already anticipated the era of the 1980s, which would be marked by increasing size and a previously unimagined diversity.

Television anchorman Sylvan Rodríguez and meteorologist Mario Gómez, two of the increasing numbers of talented Mexican Americans in Houston's mainstream media during the "Decade of the Hispanic." Photo by the author.

CHAPTER EIGHT

"Decade of the Hispanic," 1980s

SINCE THE LATE 1970S, the Houston Mexican American community has been marked by increasing size and unimagined diversity. The militancy of the preceding decade subsided considerably, and the term "Hispanic" came into vogue as a designation for Spanish-speaking people, rivaling the terms "Chicano" and "Mexican American." Such terminology attempted to incorporate the vast range of nationalities that constituted the Houston Spanish-speaking community, including individuals from all socioeconomic classes and of various Latin American ancestries. By the mid-1980s, continued growth increased the number of Houston Hispanics until an estimated five hundred thousand resided in the metropolitan area.

In many parts of the United States, people labeled the 1980s as the "Decade of the Hispanic." Conferences and organizations in Houston's Spanish-speaking community as well as other observers took up this slogan as a portent that the societal influence due them would at last be achieved. Many held to it as an optimistic sign. While Hispanic Houstonians did assume a greater role in the future direction of the city, the community remained plagued by continuing difficulties and the promise implied in the phrase remained only partially fulfilled. In short, the "Decade of the Hispanic" came and went, but positive change remained slow in coming.

To anyone who remained unaware of the presence of this sizeable subcommunity, the Torres/Moody Park episodes served as eye-openers. The diverse and burgeoning Hispanic presence could no longer be denied. The census of 1980 revealed that Houston had more than 281,321 Hispanics (17.6 percent of the city's population), ranking fifth in U.S. cities behind New York, Los Angles, Chicago, and San Antonio. Many experts believed that these figures were low, estimating the number at more than three

Car Club, 1982, by award-winning photographer Carlos Antonio Rios. This North Side lowriders organization called the "Latin Attractions" gathered for an outing at Moody Park and represented wholesome activities by ordinary people. Photo courtesy of Carlos Antonio Rios.

hundred thousand, as Hispanics have always proven difficult to record. By 1986, the sesquicentennial year of Houston's founding, market studies indicated that five hundred twenty-six thousand Hispanics lived in Harris County alone, representing roughly 20 percent of the total population. This number approximated the percentage of Hispanics statewide.

Those same market studies predicted that Houston and Harris County could well become predominantly Hispanic in the near future. Such a development seemed remarkable considering that less than five hundred Mexicans (little more than 1 percent of the city's population) had lived in Houston at the turn of the century.

People also confronted the fact that Hispanics lived in every part of the city, a pattern that had unfolded since the end of World War II. In 1979, *The Houston Post* noted fifteen major areas of Hispanic concentration. An analysis of the community during 1985–86 by Telesurveys of Texas, Inc., a Houston-based group, confirmed this demographic diversity. It found that, while Hispanics lived in numerous pockets of concentration (*barrios* of both historic and more recent origins), Hispanics were "the least residentially segregated population in Harris County." Its analysis of the

1980 census and later data revealed that Hispanics comprised at least 5 percent of the population in 80 percent of the Harris County census tracts and were relatively evenly distributed across the four quadrants of the city, illustrating a remarkable residential dispersion.

Hispanics, especially Mexican Americans, still demonstrated their vast range and complexity in terms of personal points of identification. While they still celebrated their Mexican heritage, from *fiestas patrias* celebrations to aspects of their home life, a *Houston Post* reporter interviewed a group of Mexican Americans at a local park on April 22, 1986 who wished they could be at the San Jacinto Monument to help celebrate the sesquicentennial of Sam Houston's victory over General Santa Anna. They stated that if Texas still remained a part of Mexico, "things would be a . . . lot worse." One young man opined that he only regretted that the Mexican Army had not made a better showing at the battle "for appearances' sake." These feelings demonstrated an evolution of views within the community in terms of the symbols that bound together Houstonians of all ethnicities.

Studies in the 1980s demonstrated that people of Mexican descent still constituted the majority of the Houston Hispanic community (probably eight out of ten). But the *gente* also included Puerto Ricans, Cubans, Salvadorans, and other people from South and Central America.

The 1980 census listed more than three thousand five hundred Puerto Ricans and six thousand Cubans in Harris County. Due to their relatively small numbers and high degree of assimilation, Puerto Ricans and Cubans did not comprise any identifiable residential enclaves in Houston. They did, however, add to the richness of the Hispanic presence. For example, a scholar of Puerto Rican extraction, Nicolás Kanellos, had made Houston the center for publishing Hispanic literature in the United States since 1980, at which time he brought his literary journal, *Revisita Chicano-Riqueña,* and Arte Público Press to the University of Houston.

The Cubans, as a group, entered Houston in the early 1960s in response to the revolutionary changes on their native island. By the 1980s they had generated only a handful of organizations but were the most socioeconomically well-off of the major Hispanic groups in the city. Cubans were especially well represented in business, the professions, and skilled labor. In April 1986, Reverend Enrique San Pedro, born in Havana, became auxiliary bishop of the Roman Catholic Diocese of Galveston-Houston. San Pedro's appointment took place partially in response to the large Spanish-speaking population of this area.

Central Americans made perhaps the most significant numerical addition to the diversity of Hispanics in Houston. Sociologist Nestor Rodríguez,

A Guatemalan folklore association at *fiesta patrias*, 1987, against the background of Houston's newly opened Gus S. Wortham Theater Center, illustrated the addition of other Hispanic groups to Houston's Spanish-speaking community. Photo by the author.

a keen student of the Central American community, noted that the Central American population in Houston was almost totally a phenomenon of the late 1970s and 1980s. By 1986, approximately fifty thousand Salvadorans, fifteen thousand Guatemalans, and ten thousand Hondurans made the city their place of residence. The majority (although not all) of these three groups were undocumented refugees from their respective countries' tumultuous conditions during the late 1970s and early 1980s, much as the Mexican immigrants in the post-1910 period had fled war and instability in Mexico.

Rodríguez observed that the Central Americans added a new cultural dimension to the Houston Hispanic populace. Because they shared the Hispanic culture and Spanish language, they used the traditional *barrios* as bases for settlement. But they also moved into other regions of the city to establish their own subculture. The early 1980s, for example, saw large numbers of Salvadorans settle into previously Anglo apartment complexes in the southwest part of the city to form visible, unique settlements and serve as a ready labor pool.

The Central Americans formed a large part of Houston's population of undocumented workers (or "illegal aliens"), a group that posed one of the most important contemporary issues for Hispanics in the city. The question of undocumented workers during the 1980s heated up as a complex and controversial matter, serving to point out yet again the diversity of Houston's Hispanics.

Houston became identified nationally with the subject of undocumented immigrants when, in 1977, President Jimmy Carter appointed Leonel J. Castillo, Houston's popular city controller, as director of the Immigration and Naturalization Service. As the first Mexican American ever to serve in that capacity, Castillo brought a unique sensitivity to the position, and he assumed wide recognition as an active director during his tenure.

The immigrant issue initially revolved around the thousands of undocumented Mexicans who resided in Houston by the late 1970s and filled the need for unskilled and semi-skilled labor. But many questioned whether the newcomers took jobs otherwise available to American citizens. Also, the education of the immigrants' children at state expense took center stage. State and local officials generally feared the extra costs of what they felt would be a flood of such children if public tax revenue were used to educate them.

Many people in the Houston and Anglo communities, however, felt that the financial burden to society would be even greater if these children did not receive proper schooling. Local groups sponsored privately or by churches became involved in counseling these undocumented people and their families. Several private *barrio* schools, such as the Guadalupe Aztlán School northeast of downtown and one at the Maranatha Baptist church in the Second Ward, arose to provide some elementary education for these children who lived on the fringes of society.

In July 1980, however, U.S. district judge Woodrow Seals ruled unconstitutional the state law denying non-citizens an education at public expense. In the fall of 1980, the public schools opened to the children of undocumented immigrants and, as many of their defenders had argued, no crisis erupted.

During the 1980s, the social welfare organizations in the *barrios* focused on assisting undocumented immigrants. Two *Casa De Amigos* health clinics and the Wesley Community Center in the North Side, the Chicano Family Center of Magnolia Park, and Ripley House in Second Ward, all well-established social service agencies, provided help for this bottomless well of need. Other organizations sprang up, such as *Casa Juan Diego, Communidad Oscar Romero, Communidad Bill Woods,* the Central American Refugee Committee (CRECEN), and others, to deliver social services to the undocumented. The number of lawyers, clergy, religious and social workers, and other professionals who specialized in immigration matters

Members of the staff of Casa Juan Diego, 4818 Rose Street, a grassroots social service agency for Central American refugees in Houston, 1988, demonstrated compassion and solidarity with Houston's most vulnerable residents. *Left to right:* Julio Huezo, Annemarie Renfle, Jennifer Zwick, Louise Zwick, Mark Zwick, and Antonio Butrón. Photo by the author.

expanded during the 1980s. Their attention was crucial since undocumented immigrants ranked among the most unprotected and victimized of any group in Houston society, and their lives were often filled with deprivation and fear of deportation.

The Central American refugees in Houston illustrated how connected the city was to national political currents as U.S. foreign policy after 1980 played a role in more and more people fleeing their homeland. The actions of the administration of President Ronald Reagan, which funded such repressive governments as the one in El Salvador, sent thousands north across Mexico into cities in the United States. An underground community of these refugees in sympathy with the rebels surfaced in the *barrios.* A group of people consisting of Anglos, Latinos, and African Americans of all backgrounds in solidarity with the progressive forces within Central America and opposed to Reagan and later President George H. W. Bush's policies simultaneously took form in Houston. Naturally, these individuals became targets of Houston police surveillance, a form of official harassment that long-time members of the Houston Mexican American establishment resented.

While a degree of ambivalence toward undocumented workers existed within the Hispanic community, longtime Mexican Americans could generally identify with the newcomers' struggle for survival in a hostile world. Hispanics resented criticism of the immigrants' presence when based on anti-Hispanic sentiment. Many local Mexican American groups fought passage of the controversial federal immigration legislation of the mid-1980s because, among other things, they felt it would have a negative impact upon all Hispanics in the United States. They felt especially uneasy with the provision that imposed sanctions against employers for hiring the undocumented. Such a rule, they felt, might make employers reluctant to hire any Hispanic for fear of inadvertently violating the law.

By 1986, when the U.S. Congress decided to act, an estimated seventy-five thousand undocumented Central Americans and over eighty thousand undocumented Mexicans resided in Houston. In that year, despite opposition from progressive Hispanic organizations, the U.S. Congress passed the Simpson-Rodino immigration bill, which, among other things, provided for "amnesty" for those undocumented immigrants who could prove residence before January 1982 but also levied employer sanctions. The Houston Legalization Center of the U.S. Immigration and Naturalization Service quickly became the nation's leader in drawing people to request legal status under the new law before the May 4, 1988 deadline. A total of one hundred thirty thousand people applied for amnesty in Houston, ranking the legalization office in the Bayou City as the busiest one

Undocumented residents wait in line at Houston's Immigration and Naturalization Service Legalization Center on Houston's North Side to apply for amnesty before the May 4, 1988 deadline. Photo by the author.

Houston trail riders *Los Rancheros* celebrated their *vaquero Tejano* traditions during the 1988 Houston Fat Stock Show and Rodeo. Photo by the author.

in the United States. Despite the act, undocumented people continued
arriving, as dire conditions at home and a two thousand–mile border will
always trump efforts to stop the flow of people. Undocumented Hispanic
immigration to Houston remained contentious.

The size and diversity of the Hispanic community in Houston spawned
increased excitement during the 1980s with the "Hispanic market": that is,
the potential buying power of the bicultural wage earners. In 1986, marketing studies startlingly revealed that the twenty-county area reached by
Houston's media contained more than seven hundred thousand Hispanic
residents.

Their presence contributed to the development of *El Mercado Del Sol*,
a multi-million-dollar cultural, entertainment, and retail center in the
historic *Segundo Barrio* near Guadalupe Church. *El Mercado* was a joint
venture of private and public funds developed by the administration of
Mayor Kathy Whitmire. It resulted from the construction of the nearby
convention center and was modeled on similar markets in Boston, Phil-
adelphia, Los Angeles, and San Antonio. When it opened in May 1985,
El Mercado received praise as an example of inner-city development. Its
admirers hailed it as a focal point for future activities of the Hispanic community with its retail stores and festival space. Although well designed

and attractive, financial difficulties plagued *El Mercado* almost from the start. Sadly, it closed in December 1989 when its handful of remaining merchants received eviction notices from the investors.

The proliferation of media aimed at the Spanish-speaking community represented another sign of increased attention to the Hispanic market. Radio station KEYH began broadcasting totally in Spanish in February 1979, the first to do so since the establishment of KLVL in 1950. A rivalry soon developed between KEYH and KLAT (or "*La Tremenda*"), another newcomer, for the Spanish-speaking audience. Thereafter, the number of Spanish-language radio stations increased until by mid-1986 seven competed for the market share. Spanish-language television stations KXLN-TV, Channel 45 and KTMD-TV, Channel 48 began broadcasting in Houston in 1987 and 1988, respectively, to complete the variety of electronic Hispanic-oriented media.

Also by mid-1986, seven Spanish or bilingual newspapers served the Hispanic community. Like the radio stations, the various periodicals often targeted different segments of the population: Mexican Americans, recent Mexican immigrants, Central Americans, Cubans, or South Americans. The birth and decline of numerous weekly Hispanic-oriented newspapers marked the latter part of the decade. However, *El Sol* and *El Méxica* (under the direction of Reverend James Novarro and Rogelio Noriega, respectively) remained two of the most prominent and long-lasting weeklies, both originating prior to the contemporary period. *La Voz* began publication in 1980 through the efforts of Armando and Olga Ordoñez, who came from their native Cuba via Dallas.

Other additions to the city's landscape resulted from the attention to the Hispanic market. The proliferation of Fiesta Mart supermarkets became the most notable. Begun in 1972 by non-Hispanics Donald Bonham and O. C. Mendenhall, the first gigantic store was located on the North Side and stocked foods that appealed to Hispanic tastes. By 1980, four operated, and by 1986, Fiesta Mart thrived as a chain of fourteen locations in Houston and continued to grow. The presence of a Fiesta Mart signified a contiguous concentration of Hispanic people.

Fiesta Cab Company (unaffiliated with the food stores) opened in late 1986 with bilingual drivers and a fleet of red, white, and green taxis, literally adding festive color to Houston's hectic streets. Motorists became accustomed during the 1980s to Spanish-language billboards as well as the presence of roadside shopping strips of retail stores clearly aimed at Hispanic clientele. In an effort to conform to the ethnic flavor of the community, architects began to utilize Hispanic motifs. The neo-Hispanic architectural style became more prevalent in public buildings, shopping and commercial centers, and social service agencies, especially in the north and east sides of the city. Daily reminders of the burgeoning Hispanic population in Houston seemed endless.

Houston's Hispanic political leadership became particularly influential during the 1980s. A significant milestone was reached when Ben Reyes relinquished his position in the Texas House of Representatives to become the first Mexican American member of the Houston City Council. Reyes won election in 1979 to represent the First District, which included the Mexican American north and east sides of town. He soon became one of the more forceful, progressive council members.

Albert Luna III won the special primary election in January 1980 for the seat Reyes vacated in the state legislature. He triumphed over Richard P. Holgin and Rudy Vara, two veteran political activists. Luna, twenty-nine years old at the time of his election, was a Democratic Party regular, served his district ably, and in July 1984 became chairman of the twenty-person Mexican American Legislative Caucus of the Texas House of Representatives, thus extending the voice of Hispanic Houstonians beyond the city limits.

Roman Martínez soon joined Luna as Houston's other Hispanic state representative. Martínez won the seat for the 148th District in 1982 in a hotly contested primary over Frumencio Reyes, Olga Solíz, and Gene Mendoza, three well-known personalities. Martínez was a twenty-three-year-old graduate of Yale University. In many respects, he and Luna personified a new generation of Houston Hispanic political figures.

Political campaigns within the Hispanic community were highly competitive. Various factions drew more young Hispanics into the process. The 1988 Democratic primary, for example, became the most heated election to date when Victor Treviño (a young Houston police officer and political ally of Albert Luna) narrowly defeated John E. Castillo (an ally of Ben Reyes) for the party's nomination as Precinct 6 constable. Simultaneously, the venerable Raúl Martínez, who had retired as constable of Precinct 6, unsuccessfully challenged Luna for his legislative position, which many interpreted as a countermeasure by Reyes to the Treviño race against Castillo.

Several Mexican American judges during the 1980s, including A. D. Adios, Alfred Leal, David Mendoza, and Felix Salazar, won office in countywide races. It nonetheless remained extremely difficult for Spanish-surnamed candidates in Houston to be elected in other than predominantly Hispanic districts.

State Representative Roman Martínez, 1987, personified a younger generation of Hispanic political officials. Photo by the author.

As the number of Hispanics in positions of leadership began to grow, the increasing visibility of Hispanic women represented one of the healthier developments during the 1980s. Of course, women had been active in the community since its beginnings, but their roles, with a few exceptions, were not as recognized as their contributions to the quality of life warranted. People like Janie Tijerina, Angelina Morales, María Reyna, Carmen Cortés, and many others had made their mark. Countless Mexican American women had worked tirelessly for causes and organizations, most often in the background and unheralded.

During the 1980s, more recognition came the way of these advocates. *Fiestas Patrias* honored longtime community workers Juanita Navarro and Rachel Lucas with the Distinguished Mexican American of the Year Award in 1979 and 1980, respectively. Both had labored in *barrio* organizations for many years and had set examples for younger women to emulate.

A popular singer and guitarist since the 1930s, Houstonian Lydia Mendoza began to receive the critical acclaim she so deserved. Lydia was perhaps the most important living cultural figure in the U.S. Mexican American community during the 1980s and was a legend in her own time. From her home in Houston she toured nationally and internationally, as

Houstonian Lydia Mendoza was widely acknowledged during the 1980s as a living cultural treasure. Her music dating from the 1930s reflected the feelings and sacrifices of Hispanic women and connected the past with the present. Photo courtesy of the Houston Metropolitan Research Center, Houston Public Library, Lydia Mendoza Collection.

well as sang in local neighborhood *mercados* and lounges where she could be close to Mexican American audiences who appreciated the emotional depth of her songs.

Perhaps the significant number of young professional Hispanic women on mainstream television became the most conspicuous females of the 1980s. Popular figures such as reporters Elma Barrera, Olga Campos, and Adela Gonzales, talk-show hosts Cindy Garza, Rosa Linda Pérez, and Sandy Rivera, producer/host Betti Maldonado, and anchorwoman Sylvia Pérez ranked among the Hispanic talent who became household names in the Bayou City.

Hispanic women took the lead in many community organizations. People such as Olga Soliz and Cilia Teresa of the Harris County Women's

Political Caucus, Hilda García of IMAGE, Sylvia J. García of the Hispanic
Advisory Council to the Mayor, and Mamie García, Dolores Guerrero,
María Canfield, and Margaret González of LULAC emerged as powerful
personalities in their respective groups. In the mid-1980s, Mayor Whitmire
appointed attorney Sylvia R. Garcia to be a municipal court judge. In 1987,
the mayor elevated her to the head of the city's municipal courts.

Rosie Zamora-Cope, a businesswoman, founded the Hispanic Genea-
logical Society of Houston in 1980 to help Hispanics more fully appreciate
their role in this society by understanding their past. The organization
remained vibrant throughout the decade and beyond and formed part
of the state and national network of Hispanic genealogists that practiced
solid historical inquiry, demonstrating the distinctiveness and connected-
ness of Hispanic development with the rest of Texas history. Dr. Dorothy
Caram, an educator active in several Hispanic organizations, helped to
focus young people's attention on entering the professions where they
could more fully share in Houston's economic benefits. From her position

Television reporter and media personality Elma Barrera
during the 1980s personified the rise of women in highly
visible professional positions. Photo by the author.

Mayor Kathy Whitmire (*left*) swearing in Judge Sylvia R. García as head of Houston's Municipal Courts, May 20, 1987, an event that symbolized the many advances made by Hispanic women in public office.

in the Houston Hispanic Forum, she sponsored conferences that provided information to Hispanic junior high and high school students regarding educational and career opportunities.

Many viewed Dr. Guadalupe Quintanilla, Associate Provost of the University of Houston, as representative of the numerous successful Mexican American women in higher learning. A school dropout at age fourteen, she reentered the educational system as an adult and, against much adversity, eventually earned a doctorate. Quintanilla moved beyond the campus, involving herself in a legion of civic affairs. She pioneered teaching Spanish language and Hispanic culture courses to Houston police officers. Nationally, she served for a time in the 1980s on the U.S. delegation to the United Nations during the Reagan administration.

Augustina Reyes won election to the HISD board of trustees in 1981 and again in 1983. In 1984, she became president of the board. She had formerly served as head of HISD's bilingual program and, as a school trustee, helped to add Hispanic input to the direction of the school system. Olga Gallegos joined her when she won election to the school board in 1987.

Since the 1910s, the Mexican American community viewed education as the foundation of the future. In the 1980s, Anglo-Houstonians continued to be reminded of the importance of education of the Hispanic child; figures revealed that by the fall of 1985, of the total student enrollment in HISD, over seventy thousand, or 36 percent, were Hispanic. Considering these numbers, Hispanic women, as school board members, administrators, teachers, aides, and parents, exercised a profound influence on the future course of the city.

The number of Hispanic women dramatically increased in all the professions as well as in the city's major corporations. These mainly young women dramatically represented the evolution of the Hispanic population in the Bayou City. Their grandparents may have come to Houston as immigrants and settled in the early Mexican *barrios*. Through changing cultural norms, education, and economic advancement of their parents and themselves, young women of the 1980s lived in areas previously off limits to Hispanics and conformed to the ideals of an upper-middle-class lifestyle.

Students and teachers at the George I. Sánchez High School, an alternative educational institution, 204 Clifton Street, 1986. Photo by the author.

Because Houston historically prized its entrepreneurial spirit, Hispanic women naturally took their place in commerce during the "Decade of the Hispanic." More and more women owned and operated businesses of all descriptions catering to both Hispanic and non-Hispanic markets. Many of them provided the leadership within Houston's several Hispanic and Mexican American Chambers of Commerce.

Since restaurants represented a traditional, highly visible route for Mexican Americans to enter the middle class, Ninfa Laurenzo emerged as perhaps the most recognized, distinguished Hispanic businesswoman. Ninfa, as people affectionately knew her, came originally from Harlingen, Texas, in the Rio Grande valley region. She moved to Houston with her husband in 1948, where they opened the Rio Grande Food Products Company on Navigation Boulevard in the Second Ward. They met and associated with such established entrepreneurs as Felix and Janie Tijerina. Widowed in 1969, Ninfa and her children struggled to make their business go. In 1973, they converted a portion of their company's building into a small restaurant. "Ninfa's" soon grew in popularity to become a Bayou City phenomenon—a favorite spot to get her special kind of Mexican food.

In 1976, they opened their second Ninfa's on Westheimer adjacent to fashionable southwestern subdivisions, and thereafter they expanded until, by May 1981, they operated seven locations in Houston, one in San Antonio, and three in Dallas. Throughout the 1980s, they became the "in-place" to eat, much as Felix Mexican Restaurants had during the late 1940s and 1950s. In 1981, Ninfa was named national businesswoman of the year by the United States Hispanic Chamber of Commerce. The following year, the Houston Theater Under the Stars produced *Ninfa!*, an original musical play based on her life.

As she rose in prominence, Ninfa became active in the community, participating in a variety of charitable endeavors. In 1977, she was appointed to the board of the Metropolitan Transit Authority (MTA) and raised support for the MTA in the *barrios*. As a familiar figure in the Houston media for the next decade, she became a symbol of Houston Hispanics in the 1980s.

The women who came into their own by the 1980s possessed the common denominator of having a broader commitment to community affairs. They involved themselves in more than self-betterment. Rather they saw community involvement as an extension of their work—a way to contribute to the greater good as a necessary part of their lives.

Despite positive developments, however, traditional problems still existed for Hispanics. A high rate of school dropouts, lower-than-average educational attainment, a median income level well below that of main-stream Houston, underrepresentation in positions of authority, and a greater chance that they as individuals would be touched by crime and violence were just a few of the conditions that demonstrated that being Hispanic in Houston generally meant to be less well-off than most residents. Much more needed to be accomplished in Houston to realize the promises inherent in the 1980s phrase "Decade of the Hispanic."

Residential indication of the massive expansion of the Hispanic community into the suburbs, where apartment complexes and subdivisions catered to Spanish-speaking newcomers by the 1990s. Photo by the author.

CHAPTER NINE

Toward the New Millennium

DURING THE 1990S, Hispanics living in Houston figuratively made their way toward another century and a new millennium. Likewise, thousands of other Spanish-speaking people migrated to the Bayou City. Growth and diversity remained the order of the day. From approximately four hundred fifty thousand Hispanics in Houston proper in 1990, the community rose to over seven hundred thirty thousand by 2000, with Mexican Americans remaining the majority within this population. Hispanics (of various national backgrounds) became Houston's largest ethnic group, making for the Latinizing of the metropolis. By 2000, the Bayou City ranked fourth in the nation behind New York, Los Angeles, and Chicago in the number of Hispanic residents. Houston had nudged out San Antonio for this standing.

The 1990 U.S. census determined that Hispanics made up 27.6 percent of Houston's entire population. They rivaled African Americans, whose numbers placed them at approximately 27.5 percent. The 1990 census also showed Hispanics as becoming the city's fastest growing ethnic group. This trend starkly manifested itself ten years later. In the 2000 census, a whopping 37.4 percent of Houstonians were Latino, by then outstripping the 25.3 percent who were black. Hispanics were the numerically dominant ethnicity in what had begun as a southern city where African Americans had historically held that position.

The salient issues facing the Hispanic community emanated in part from this massive expansion. To a large measure, these problems were the same as before: education, political representation, a decent standard of living, the plight of undocumented immigrants, cultural acceptance, and inclusion as fully participating urban dwellers. Like the preceding "Decade of the Hispanic," the 1990s held promise but also shortcomings.

However, Houstonians had grown accustomed to and even embraced this tremendous Hispanic presence as the new millennium dawned.

Acquiring an education remained a chief focus for Hispanics, and their large numbers within the school system called for attention. In 1990 Hispanics comprised approximately 43 percent of the student body of the HISD, compared to 40 percent black enrollment. By January 1990, Hispanic students outnumbered any other ethnic population in HISD for the first time.

Regardless of advances made in previous decades, educators noted that most of the problems for Hispanic students persisted to one degree or another. Various coalitions formed in response to what observers saw as dilapidated and overcrowded conditions in Hispanic-majority schools. These voices pushed for hiring more Hispanic teachers and having smaller classes. Advocates included local educators such as University of Houston administrator Lorenzo Cano (brother of veteran educator Luis Cano) and Professor Guadalupe San Miguel Jr. of the University of Houston, community spokespeople such as W. R. Morris, concerned parents, and many others. They studied the issues and petitioned the HISD Board of Trustees to address the trouble spots. Hispanic activists even grumbled at the Houston Community College System (HCCS) for deficiencies in the selection of Hispanic administrators for the HCCS.

Although people debated what constituted the "dropout rate" among Hispanic students, everyone agreed that it was unacceptably high. Even HISD studies during the decade found that 40 percent of its Hispanic ninth graders would leave school before they graduated.

Those pupils who earned their high school diplomas found opportunity at area colleges and universities, including branch campuses of the University of Houston, Houston Community College, San Jacinto College, and other area institutions of higher learning. Dr. Tatcho Mindiola Jr. and Lorenzo Cano, director and associate director, respectively, of the University of Houston Center for Mexican American Studies, stood out for their efforts to encourage students to further their education.

The HISD Board of Trustees consisted of nine members in July 1990, but only two were Hispanic. Tina Reyes, a pioneer on the board, resigned from her position in February 1990. Félix Fraga, the venerable director of Ripley House, filled her spot first through appointment and then by election, serving with trustee Olga Gallegos as the other Hispanic voice on the board. In 1994, Esther Campos, a 37-year veteran of civic activity on Houston's East Side, won election as HISD trustee to succeed Fraga, who pursued higher office.

Dr. Tatcho Mindiola Jr., director of the University of Houston Center for Mexican American Studies, along with associate director Lorenzo Cano, personified the Chicano intellectual presence in Houston's institutions of higher learning during the final decades of the twentieth century. Photo courtesy of the University of Houston Center for Mexican American Studies.

After much wrangling by advocates, Gabriel Vásquez became the third Hispanic member on the school board. By 1999, Olga Gallegos, Esther Campos, and Vásquez were the three Hispanic trustees; many saw this number as representing Latino parity.

Alternative schools remained a Houston feature, the most significant of which continued to be AAMA, with its George I. Sánchez Charter High School. In 1998, the school had 500 students and focused mainly on at-risk Hispanic pupils. In July 1999, the school opened a thirty-one thousand square foot addition. Vice President and presidential candidate Albert Gore attended the dedication. This expansion allowed for a significant growth of the student body.

Located along the Gulf Freeway, the impressive AAMA facility had more than 100,000 square feet of educational space by the end of the decade. Its high school boasted a computer lab with connection to the Internet, impressive library, science laboratory, cafeteria, gymnasium, and daycare for students with small children. AAMA also offered evening adult education; the program included classes where hopefuls could prepare to take the GED and to improve their English language skills. AAMA created a community development corporation with a moderate-sized apartment complex that provided housing for working families. Extending its mission even further afield, AAMA opened branch centers in San Antonio, Edinburg, Weslaco, and Laredo.

The Hispanic community remained a beehive of political jockeying among Hispanic rivals and races against Anglo opponents. Leaders clamored for more representation in every level of government. So complex (and contentious) did the political scene become that the treatment that follows only skims the surface.

As the new decade began, many observers—Mexican Americans, blacks, and Anglos alike—saw City Council member Ben T. Reyes as the "godfather" of Houston Hispanic politics. Viewed by supporters as a committed community activist and by adversaries as one who played hardball, Machiavellian *patrón* politics, the figure of Ben Reyes loomed large. His allies often became enemies and then once again found themselves gravitating back to his camp, prompting an astute scholar of the local scene to comment that one needed a score card to keep pace with the byzantine alliances. All agreed, however, that no one knew city politics better than Ben Reyes.

The new decade commenced with these shifting loyalties. In 1990, Al Luna vacated his seat in the Texas legislature. By then he had long since been on the outs with Reyes, his former friend and mentor, as evidenced by the bitter 1988 primary election. To fill Luna's 143th District position, another heated political tussle occurred in the Democratic primary when Mario Gallegos, a Reyes protégé, Houston firefighter, and son of school board member Olga Gallegos, contested Mike Moreno, a Luna-backed candidate. Gallegos emerged triumphant, but many viewed the squabbling between the Reyes and Luna factions as detrimental to the Hispanic community's forward progress.

In 1991, Houston Hispanic politicos, spearheaded by Representative Román Martínez, succeeded in the Texas legislature in gerrymandering what they considered would be a Hispanic district for the U.S. House of Representatives. This new seat, the Twenty-Ninth District, included parts of the north, east, and southeast sides of Houston where a Hispanic majority resided, making the district approximately 60 percent Latino. Although a number of candidates eyed the new post, the 1992 primary featured Ben Reyes and state senator Gene Green, an Anglo and veteran of twenty years in state government, in a hotly contested runoff.

Although Reyes had edged out Green in the first round, Green defeated Reyes by 180 votes in the runoff. A ruling by a state district judge overturned the election results, giving Reyes another opportunity. In the re-vote, Green again emerged victorious. Green went on to defeat Reyes in the 1994 primary and subsequently defeated other Mexican American hopefuls who tried to unseat him for what had been initially envisioned as a Hispanic post.

In that same 1992 runoff, by-then five-term state representative Román Martínez also went down in defeat, losing to incumbent state senator John Whitmire in a mud-slinging campaign for newly created Fifteenth Senate District. Although they had their detractors even among Hispanic voters and had faced seasoned opponents, the defeat of Reyes and Martínez represented symbolic reversals for Hispanics. The fact that longtime political activist Frumencio Reyes and the Harris County Mexican American Democrats had endorsed Whitmire over Martínez simply underscored the complicated nature, growing sophistication, and acrimoniousness of local Latino politics.

In 1994, an intense election for the Sixth Senate District took place between former state representative Román Martínez and sitting two-term state representative Mario Gallegos. The winner would become the city's first Hispanic in the Texas Senate. Gallegos won the primary and in November took that seat, thus making Houston Hispanic political history.

The political bombshell of the decade exploded, however, with the downfall of Ben Reyes. Reyes had left the city council in December 1995 because of term limitations, ending his tenure in elective office that extended back to 1972. In 1997, federal authorities indicted him for bribery and conspiracy. An FBI sting operation charged Reyes with a scheme to purchase the votes of several City Council members on a quid pro quo for constructing the massive convention center hotel project in downtown Houston.

After one deadlocked jury, a retrial found Reyes guilty in 1998, and the following year he began serving a sentence of nine years in federal prison. It amounted to a tragic chapter in the career of a political figure recognized even by his strident adversaries as a man of commitment to and compassion for his constituents, especially the poor to whom he had delivered many humanitarian services. Equally lamentable, the personable media entrepreneur Betti Maldonado, who in 1994 had become the first Hispanic woman Houston port commissioner, was also convicted of involvement in the payoffs and went to jail, a tragedy that curtailed her career.

Other Hispanics won election to the Houston City Council. In 1991, Gracie Saenz became the first Hispanic woman to win a Houston City

Council at-large position, joining Ben Reyes and Felix Fraga (the latter elected in 1993 for District H, a predominantly Hispanic district) on that governmental body. Saenz gained re-election in 1993. Orlando Sánchez, a Republican of Cuban descent and former probation officer, won in 1995 as the second Hispanic at-large City Council member. He was opposed by the Harris County Mexican American Democrats. Sánchez had received backing from archconservatives like Congressman Tom DeLay and other opponents of affirmative action. With Reyes out of office and the election of John E. Castillo in 1995, four Hispanics (among a total of fourteen members) served on the city council. Gabriel Vásquez, who had been on the school board, succeeded Fraga as a City Council member for District H in 2000.

While most high-level political hopefuls were male, Hispanic women also sought political office. Sylvia García, chief of Houston's municipal court system since 1987, staged an unsuccessful primary bid for the U.S. House of Representatives in 1992 and then in 1996 fell short in her race for Harris County Attorney. In 1997, she nonetheless ran for and won election to the office of City Controller, a position that Leonel J. Castillo held in the 1970s.

By the end of the decade, Hispanic women flexed their political muscles in so many ways that it is difficult to enumerate. In July 1999, for instance, women in Houston organized Latina PAC, a political action committee that pursued goals such as financing Hispanic female candidates for elected office, getting them appointed to commissions and boards in increased numbers, providing guidance and mentoring to young Latinas on local university campuses, and generally trying to forge unity and effectiveness on health care, economic development, education, and other issues concerning women.

By 1999, the list of women in positions of leadership in the professions and civic arenas also became almost too long to detail. Comprising much of the membership of community organizations, they turned their attentions to assisting other aspiring Hispanics, female and male.

Houston always took pride in its reputation as an entrepreneurial city, and Hispanic achievement buttressed that reputation. In 1991, studies reported that Houston ranked fourth in the nation in the number of Hispanic-owned companies, nudging San Antonio, which came in fifth. Houston contained almost sixteen thousand such firms.

The Hispanic Chamber of Commerce continued to be a force in the economic affairs of the city during the 1990s, hosting annual fundraising black-tie events that celebrated established as well as rising businesspeople. The Chamber fostered Hispanic entrepreneurs who would broaden the Latino middle class and solidify the community's economic base.

Crowd scene in Guadalupe Park in *El Segundo Barrio* illustrates the massive numbers of residents that comprised the growing "Hispanic market" to which businesses catered by the 1990s. Photo by the author.

As the number of female entrepreneurs increased, two indomitable businesswomen who epitomized earlier eras passed from the scene in the 1990s. Angelina Morales, who with her husband Felix had operated the longtime funeral home and radio station KLVL in the Second Ward, died in 1994, active almost until the end of her life at 87 years of age. In 1997, well into her eighties, Mrs. Felix (Janie) Tijerina also died, still operating her restaurant, a Houston institution, near the corner of Westheimer Road and Montrose Boulevard.

After much success during the 1970s and 1980s, the Ninfa's Mexican Restaurant chain sold to another restaurant group in 1997. Although no longer controlling the destiny of the establishments she had made famous, Ninfa Laurenzo, the symbol of Hispanic entrepreneurship in Houston for many residents, remained a spokesperson for the operation for the rest of the decade. (She would die in 2001 at 77, mourned by thousands at her funeral.)

Meanwhile, the ranks of the recently arrived undocumented workers continued to soar. During the mid 1990s, the number of persons applying for citizenship skyrocketed. In 1994, for example, applications doubled over what they had been the year before. People sought permanent residency through two avenues: the 1986 amnesty bill and a new program by the Immigration and Naturalization Service that tried to replace "green card" status (which apparently had more than a dozen variations) with a more universal form or even citizenship. The presence of undocumented folks was most pronounced in the suburbs, where they settled in apartment complexes. Entire suburban neighborhoods took on an increasing Hispanic flavor. Immigrant enclaves expanded and new ones emerged in most outlying regions. Such places as convenience stores sold cell phones to call Mexico and Central America, cashed paychecks, provided easy remittances of money to relatives south of the Rio Grande, and offered other services that catered to recent arrivals. Spanish so predominated that the divide between Houston and the international border seemed to have narrowed.

Although most of the undocumented simply sought honest employment, a percentage of them caused problems with the police, constables, and sheriff's department. Random lawlessness, shootings and stabbings, disreputable *cantinas,* and attendant vice that catered to the newcomers spread. By the mid 1990s, the numbers of these lawbreakers in local jails climbed to around a thousand monthly. Immigration and Naturalization Service officers in Houston found their resources overwhelmed. This bad situation alarmed city officials and residents with legitimate worries over crime and the strain it placed on city services. It unfortunately also fueled the more vociferous anti-immigrant elements in the city, who called for "sealing" the southern border. In addition, the proliferation of Hispanic youth gangs in Houston reflected the alarming presence of such criminal syndicates across the nation.

Groups like the Gulfton Area Neighborhood Organization (GANO) and Central American Refugee Center, located in southwest Houston, arose in the 1990s to combat the most extreme forms of anti-immigrant sentiment. While immigration is a complex issue, one could only empathize with the courage and perseverance of people struggling to make a living. For me, the stout-heartedness of the undocumented immigrant from Mexico manifested itself in a young man I encountered by the side of the highway near Catarina, a tiny hamlet in deep Southwest Texas. He said he was on his way to Houston. I told him it was very far, to which he replied, "Yes, but I have a job waiting for me there."

Such desperate, determined people had no more stalwart a voice during the 1990s than Houstonian María Jiménez. Perhaps the most enduring, seasoned, and admirable civic activist in the city's history, Jiménez could well merit a biography of her own.

A veteran of community causes, Jiménez was born in Coahuila, Mexico but immigrated with her family to the United States in 1957, when she was only seven years old. After settling his family in Houston's East Side,

María Jiménez (*fourth from left*), Houston community organizer, stands with a delegation from Redford, Texas during their 1997 stay in Washington, DC to call attention to the ill-advised border policy that led to the death of Esequiel Hernández Jr. *Left to right:* Enrique Madrid, Ruby Madrid, Belén Hernández, María Jiménez, Jesús Valenzuela, Dianna Valenzuela, and Rev. Melvin La Follette. Photo courtesy of María Jiménez.

María's father opened a machine shop. María descended from Mexican union organizers on both sides of her family. Since childhood she heard talk on class differences, poverty, and the inequality that existed in society. She attended Milby High School, where she became a champion debater.

As noted in Chapter 7, Jiménez attended the University of Houston, where she was a MAYO member and leader in student government and later the *Raza Unida* Party. She ran for elective office under the *Raza Unida* banner against Ben Reyes, the Democrat. In the 1970s, she relocated to Mexico. She lived there for more than a decade, engaging in grassroots civic and union activity. In 1985, she came back Houston. In 1987, Jiménez became local director of the American Friends Service Committee, a Quaker human rights group, as deeply committed as ever to the underprivileged.

By the mid 1990s, people identified Jiménez as the premier defender of immigrant rights as she led various protests around town. In 1996, she helped to organize a march in Washington and at that event addressed over ten thousand Hispanics for Latino and immigrant concerns.

In 1997, Jiménez got involved in the controversy over the death of Esequiel Hernández Jr., an innocent high school student shot mistakenly by U.S. Marines on patrol near the West Texas border town of Redford, one of the most tragic results of the "war on drugs." In trying to turn that atrocious incident into something constructive for society, Jiménez met with residents in Redford and led a delegation of bereaved family and community people to Washington, DC, where they spoke to generals at the Pentagon. As a result, the military greatly limited its use of armed personnel to interdict drugs, recognizing the explosive nature of such a practice.

In 1998, Jiménez helped a small group of Houston residents protest the shooting by police of Pedro Oregón Navarro. She became equally passionate in 1999 over the plight of an immigrant woman forced by the Harris County Hospital District to seek dialysis treatment in Mexico.

In 1998, Jiménez assumed dual nationality (which the Mexican government offered at that time), underscoring her ties to Mexico as well as her desire to effect change on both sides of the border. She participated as a monitor in the presidential elections of Mexico and provided testimony on various issues to congressional committees in both the United States and Mexico.

By the end of the decade, this champion for peace and justice remained as committed as ever to the cause of the poor. Jiménez epitomized those intelligent people who could have gained worldly riches but chose a true path of community activism. She elected to struggle for the disadvantaged. Her life illustrated that during times of change, the most fundamental issues in the struggle for justice remain the same.

Hispanics continued to celebrate their culture before the larger urban scene. As in the past, they observed such holidays as *Cinco de Mayo* and *Diez y Seis*. The *Cinco de Mayo* festivities saw a proliferation of venues during the decade. In 1993, for example, minor celebrations occurred in places from schools to restaurants to the roof of the Galleria shopping mall, where people enjoyed a swank *"Noche Latina."* At the same time, an impressive *"Cinco* in the Square Celebration" took place in Houston's old downtown Market Square to raise money for that site's revitalization. An even-larger evening event transpired at Miller Outdoor Theater in Hermann Park.

In 1995, a coalition of strong neighborhood organizations celebrated *Cinco de Mayo* in Moody Park, the first such event since the riot seventeen years before. That same year an elaborate downtown *Cinco de Mayo* parade, sponsored by the local LULAC, took place, an activity usually reserved for September 16.

Diez y Seis was set within the larger Hispanic Heritage Month in September and October. The *Fiestas Patrias* parade downtown on Saturday traditionally served as its highlight, drawing an audience from across town. In 2000, eight countries of the Hispanic world celebrated jointly their days of independence in the September 16 parade, including Mexico, Guatemala, El Salvador, Honduras, Costa Rica, Chile, Belize, and Nicaragua.

The leadership of Houston's Tejano Association for Historical Preservation prepares for the organization's first annual Cesar Chavez Day Parade, April 2000. *Front row, seated left to right*: Richard Pérez, board member; Benny C. Martínez, president; and Linda Alonzo Saenz, secretary; *middle row, standing left to right*: Margarito "Gunny" Vásquez, board member; unidentified person; Dan Martínez, member; unidentified person; and Genaro Flores, board member; *back row, standing left to right*: unidentified person; Macario Ramírez, board member; unidentified person; and Loretta Martínez Williams, co-secretary. Photo courtesy of Loretta Martínez Williams.

During the 1990s, the Houston-based Tejano Association for Historical Preservation (TAHP) was particularly active. Founded in 1989 by Rolando Romo and others, this group held regular meetings that featured learned speakers, created historical markers that focused on the local Hispanic past, and generally raised the community's historical consciousness regarding Tejanos. Its cadre of advocates also added a consideration of Hispanics to mainstream history organizations. In 2000, TAHP, led by President Benny Martinez, succeeded in renaming Sixty-Seventh Street in honor of the legendary labor leader Cesar Chávez.

Historians long since recognized that the cowboy of Western lore traced its roots to Tejano origins between the Nueces River and the Rio Grande. Given the growing numbers of Mexican Americans and their purchasing power, the people who staged the Houston Livestock Show and Rodeo appealed directly to this growing population with a Go Tejano Day.

Founded in 1987, the Go Tejano Committee was organized by members of the Hispanic community, with Eduardo Aguirre, a banker and Cuban-born Houstonian, serving as its first chairman. It struggled to attract sizeable numbers, but in the 1990s, that changed dramatically. The Go Tejano Day Committee, headed then by Tony Bruni, a longtime media producer, began to achieve real success. By 1994, Go Tejano Day became one of the most well-attended events in the rodeo's weeklong festivities at the Astrodome.

Go Tejano Day received a major boost when the committee booked performers who appealed directly to the young Hispanic music consumer. In 1993, Selena Quintanilla of Corpus Christi, the reigning queen of *Tejano* music, came as the headliner. She drew a record crowd of almost fifty-eight thousand for her matinee appearance. She again starred in 1994 and 1995 to even larger audiences, just before her untimely death in late March of that latter year. In 1996, acts such as *Oscar de la Rosa & La Mafia* and *La Diferenzia* filled this void. In 1998, Go Tejano Day attracted a crowd of approximately one hundred thirty-two thousand. In 1999, under Go Tejano Committee chairwoman Marie Arcos, the attendance stayed consistent at around one hundred thirty-one thousand. Like those before it, the 1999 day had a distinctly Hispanic flavor, with a mariachi competition inside the Astrodome and with musical performances by Emilio, David Lee Garza, Ram Herrera, and other *Tejano* personalities.

Go Tejano Day and its committee had as its sole objective raising money for scholarships for Hispanic students. In 1993, for instance, the day garnered $160,000 for this purpose; in 1996, it raised $300,000; in 1999, it topped over $600,000. Once again, these efforts underscored the community's commitment to education.

Media catering to the Hispanic audience likewise continued to proliferate. Among the prime examples, Azteca América in October 2000 started broadcasting in Houston, making it the third Spanish-language television station. It competed with Univisión and Telemundo. These venues sat atop the numerous other forms of mass communication and Spanish-language marketing forms, from radio stations to the ubiquitous billboards to bilingual labels on store shelves.

As Houston ended the twentieth century, people came to terms with the idea that no specific magic year would see the resolution of all problems for Houston's Hispanics. History has demonstrated that Hispanics had achieved their gains through an evolutionary process, by such things as changing laws and attitudes, education, hard work, luck, a little help from one another and their non-Hispanic friends, and, of course, sheer

Luis Cano and Tony Bruni, active in many aspects of
Houston's Hispanic community and shown here in
vaquero attire, played seminal roles in the development of Go Tejano Day for the Houston Fat Stock
Show and Rodeo during the last decade of the twentieth century. Photo by the author.

individual determination. Moreover, problems will always exist, as is the
case with all people. The nature of a group's difficulties will be peculiar to
its own circumstances.

Even the constant refrain from Hispanics themselves that they must
achieve "unity of action" is doubtless an unreasonable expectation. Given
their historical development as a diverse group, Hispanics will have, more
often than not, diverging goals and viewpoints, thus preventing collective
action. Many Mexican Americans even find the term "Hispanic" itself
unsuitable because it reflects the conservative temper of the 1980s, when
it came into wide use. They feel that this broad definition stymies legitimate political demands by diluting their ranks with more affluent, conservative groups.

Hispanics in Houston truly represented a twentieth-century community with nineteenth-century antecedents. But this Hispanic populace, with Mexican Americans as its majority, continued to develop as a multi-faceted entity with both similarities and differences among its various members, from the recent immigrant to the most acculturated upper-middle-class resident. They also exhibited commonalities and contrasts with other Houstonians, who faced the difficult task of living in the urban wilderness that the Bayou City can be. They shared with others the many problems to which adequate solutions probably do not exist. Nonetheless, Houston's Hispanic community continued to grow in size and influence, full of vital and interesting people whose presence indelibly marks the city.

Appendix

THE FOLLOWING INDIVIDUALS, who may not be noted elsewhere in the book, have informed my understanding of Houston's Hispanic history. I deeply appreciate their valuable assistance. As participants in the development of this community, they have shared their insights and experiences with me, helped locate and identify many of the visuals, and enhanced the quality of *Del Pueblo*. I apologize if I have omitted anyone who has contributed.

Rafael Acosta
David Adame
Guillermo Aguayo
Mr. and Mrs. William Aguilar
Sammie Alderete
John Aleman
Johnny Almendarez
Frank and Ventura Alonzo
J. A. Tony Alvarez Jr.
Richard Ante
Robert Ante
Thomas Ante
Dario M. Arellano
Arnold Arevalo
Alex Arroyos
Petra Ayala
Judge A. D. Azios
Gonzalo Balderas
Susan and David Banda
Ruth Bello

Mary Beltran
George H. Benavides
Yolanda Garza Birdwell
Francisco Blasco
Mike Bocanegra
Orlando Boudini
Frank Brett
Tony Bruni
Daniel Bustamante
Carlos Calbillo
Eddie Canales
Arnulfo Cantú
Mel Cantú
Dr. Dorothy Caram
Rene Cardenas
Frank Carrion
Juan Carrion
Mary Ann Carrion
Lupe Casares
Mrs. Maria Casiano

Mr. and Mrs. A. John Castillo
Mr. and Mrs. Augustine Castillo Sr.
Augustine Castillo Jr.
John E. Castillo
Paul M. Castillo
Raul and Katy Castillo
Mrs. Janie Castro
Leo Cavazos
Dr. Ninfa Cavazos
Abel Cisneros
Frank Colmenero
Robert D. Contreras
Tony Contreras
Manuel Cordoba
John Coronado
Mrs. Carmen Cortes
Louis Crespo
Manuel Crespo
Hector Cruz
Lauro Cruz
Toni Davenport
Harry G. Daves Jr.
Mr. and Mrs. Atanacio P. Davila
Daniel Davila
Raul De Anda
Frank De La Cruz
Rt. Rev. Msgr. Teodoro De La Torre
Felix Del Valle
Ben Díaz
Kathryn Díaz
Martha Díaz
Porfirio and Nora Díaz
Ernest Eguía
Juanita Elizondo
Luis Escareño
Jose Maria Escobar
Mary Alice Escobedo
Arturo Eureste
Ramon Fernández
A. P. Flores

Genaro Flores
Hector Flores
Manuel Flores
Roberto Flores
Angel Z. Fraga
Felix Fraga
Rt. Rev. Msgr. Anton J. Frank
Maria Fuentes
Augustine Gabino
Ed Gaida
Adrian Galano
Alberto Gallegos
Dolores Gallegos
Leo Gallegos
Olga Gallegos
Sara Gallo
Israel Galvan
E. J. García
Fred García
Hector García
Hector J. García
Mr. and Mrs. Isidro García
John and Connie García
Mrs. Lupe García
Mamie García
Mickey García
Monico García
Mr. and Mrs. Ray García
Sal García
Sylvia J. García
Sylvia R. García
Ted García
Cindy Garza
David L. Garza
Lorenzo Garza
Gilbert Gómez
Refugio Gómez
Carmen González
Danny González
Mr. and Mrs. Elias González

Margaret González
Victor González
George and Hanifa Guido
Petra Guillen
Eddie Gutiérrez
John Gutiérrez
Linda Gutiérrez
Patricio Gutiérrez
Joyce Herrera Harper
David Heredia
Judge Alfred J. Hernández
Daniel Hernández
Johnny P. Hernández
Jose Felipe Hernández
Juan C. Hernández
Toby Hernández
Mrs. Carmen Herrera
Douglas M. Herrera
John J. Herrera
John M. Herrera
Kathy Herrera
Mike Herrera
Richard P. Holgín
Edward Ibarra
Larry Ibarra
Dick Jaffe
Deanna Jaime
Mr. and Mrs. Rudy Jasso
María Jiménez
Charlotte Kitowski, CDP
Kevin Ladd
Joel Lara
Jenny R. Laurenzo
Judge Alfred Leal
Maria Longoria
Eduardo López
Halima López
Hermilo López-Bassols
Janie López
Lola López

Rachel Lucas
Bert Luna
Betti Maldonado
Maria Marcaccio
Domingo Márquez
Benny Martínez
Eduardo Martínez
Eva, Felix, and Raul C. Martínez
Roman Martínez
Mr. and Mrs. A. L. Matta
Elsie McKenzie
Jesús Medel, ATM
Rachel Medellin
Marcos Mena
Eugene Mendoza
Lydia Mendoza
Luis Mier
Vincent G. Mindiola
Mary Lou Miranda
Mr. and Mrs. Raul Molina
Phil Montalbo
Mr. and Mrs. Felix H. Morales
Rudy Morales
Marta Moreno
Ralph Moreno
W. R. Morris
Frances Muñoz
Ben Murillo
Mrs. Jesús Murillo
Ray Murillo
Ernest Navarro
Pete Navarro
Ernest Nieto
Santos and Ester Nieto
P. L. Niño
Rogelio Noriego
Rev. James Novarro
Joe Orlando
Ben Olguín
Carlos Ordoñez

Olga Ordoñez
Joe Orlando
Frank Orozco
David Ortiz
Frank Ortiz
Chris Pérez
Cisto Pérez
Eloy Pérez
Locadio Pérez
Paul Pérez
Richard Pérez
Frank Pinedo
Diego Pino
Sister Theresa J. Powers, CDP
Maria Puente
Guillermo Pulido
Felix and Herminia Quiñones
Dr. Guadalupe Quintanilla
Mr. and Mrs. Abraham Ramírez
Arturo Ramírez
Felix and Lena Ramírez
Gloria Ramírez
Macario Ramírez
Jose Ramón
Augustina Reyes
Ben T. Reyes
Mrs. Estella Gómez Reyes
Ismael Reyes
Gilberto Rico
Jaime Rivera
Armando and Rita Rodríguez
Juvencio Rodríguez
Moses Rodríguez
Rudolph Rodríguez
Sylvan Rodríguez
Tommy Rojas
Joe Rojo
Poncho Ruíz
Gracie Saenz
Linda Alonzo Saenz

Mrs. Fernando Sálas A.
A. D. Salazar
Judge Felix Salazar
Dr. Luis Salinas
Moe Sánchez
Teresa Sánchez
Mrs. Catalina Gómez Sandoval
Alfredo Sarabia
Valentina Sarabia
Pablo Segura
Olga Solíz
Roy Solíz
Rachel Tamayo
Leo Tanguma
Cilia Teresa
Mrs. Felix Tijerina
Victoria Tijerina
Jerry Torres
Joe I. Torres
Joe Torres
Mrs. Lupe Torres
Frank C. Urteaga
George Valdez
Mrs. Cruz Valdez
Olivia Valdez
Gregorio Torres Valerio
Lea Valerio
Luz Vara
Richard Vara
Al Varela
Alfonso Vázquez
Al Vera
Augustin Villagomez
Mary Villagomez
Ralph Villagomez
Rosie Zamora-Cope
Al Zarzana
Elizabeth Zermeno
Mark and Louise Zwick

Sources for Further Reading

Yolanda Broyles-González, *Lydia Mendoza's Life in Music: La Historia de Lydia Mendoza* (Oxford and New York: Oxford University Press, 2001).

Luis Rey Cano, "Pachuco Gangs in Houston: A Postwar Phenomenon," *Agenda: A Journal of Hispanic Issues* 9, no. 1 (January/February 1979).

Marie Dauplaise, "Houston's Latin American," *Houston Chronicle* (eleven part series), December 1–11, 1958.

Arnoldo De León, *Ethnicity in the Sunbelt: A History of Mexican Americans in Houston* (College Station: Texas A&M University Press, 2001).

———. *They Called Them Greasers: Anglo Attitudes toward Mexicans in Texas, 1821–1900* (Austin: University of Texas Press, 1983).

Sam Houston Dixon and Louis Wiltz Kemp, *The Heroes of San Jacinto* (Houston: Anson Jones Press, 1931).

Carlos B. Gil, "Lydia Mendoza: Houstonian and First Lady of Mexican American Song," *Houston Review* III, no. 2 (Summer 1981).

Luis G. Gómez, *Crossing the Rio Grande: An Immigrant's Life in the 1880s,* ed. Guadalupe Valdez Jr. and Thomas H. Kreneck (College Station: Texas A&M University Press, 2008).

Mary Ellen Goodman et al., "The Mexican-American Population of Houston, A Survey in the Field, 1965–1970," *Rice University Studies* 57, no. 3 (Summer 1971).

Telesurveys of Texas, Inc., *Hispanics in Harris County* (Houston, August 1986).

"Houston's 'Little Mexico' Is a City Within a City," *Houston Chronicle,* November 9, 1930.

Thomas H. Kreneck, "Documenting a Mexican American Community: The Houston Example," *The American Archivist* 48, no. 3 (Summer 1985).

———. "Jesus Murillo: Social Artist for the Houston-Galveston Region," *The Houston Review* III, no. 2 (Summer 1981).

———. "The Letter From Chapultepec," *The Houston Review* III, no. 2 (Summer 1981).

———. *Mexican American Odyssey: Felix Tijerina, Entrepreneur and Civic Leader, 1905–1965* (College Station: Texas A&M University Press, 2001).

Margarita Melville, "Mexicans," in *The Ethnic Groups of Houston,* ed. Fred R. von der Mehden (Houston: Rice University Press, 1984).

Tatcho Mindiola Jr., "A Personal Comment on Assimilation," *The Houston Review* III, no. 2 (Summer 1981).

Chrystel K. Pit, "Deal with Us: The Business of Mexican Culture in Post-World War II Houston" (Ph.D. diss., University of Arizona, 2011).

Marilyn Rinehart and Thomas H. Kreneck, "'In the Shadow of Uncertainty': Texas Mexicans and Repatriation in Houston During the Great Depression," *The Houston Review* X, no. 1 (1988).

———. "The Minimum Wage March of 1966: A Case Study in Mexican-American Politics, Labor, and Identity," *The Houston Review* XI, no. 1 (1989).

Nestor P. Rodríguez, "Undocumented Central Americans in Houston: Diverse Populations," *International Migrations Review* (Spring 1987).

F. Arturo Rosales, "Mexicans in Houston: The Struggle to Survive, 1908–1975," *The Houston Review* III, no. 2 (Summer 1981).

———. "The Mexican Immigrant Experience in Chicago, Houston, and Tucson: Comparisons and Contrasts," in *Houston: A Twentieth Century Urban Frontier,* eds. Barry J. Kaplan and F. Arturo Rosales (Port Washington, NY, 1983).

Guadalupe San Miguel Jr., *Brown, Not White: School Integration and the Chicano Movement in Houston* (College Station: Texas A&M University Press, 2001).

Lydia Mendoza: A Family Autobiography. Compiled and introduced by Chris Strachwitz, with James Nicolopulos (Houston: Arte Público Press, 1993).

Roberto R. Treviño, *The Church in the Barrio: Mexican American Ethno-Catholicism in Houston* (Chapel Hill: The University of North Carolina Press, 2006).

Sister Mary Paul Valdez, "The History of the Missionary Catechists of Divine Providence" (N.P., 1978).

Index

Thomas, Albert, 81
Tijerina, Felix, 45, 58, 70–72, 86
Tijerina, Jane, 70–71, 119, 133
Tijerina, Reies López, 89
Torres, Albino, 36
Torres, Joe Campos, 104–106
Torres, José, 94*f*
Tovar, Henry, 64
Treviño, Roberto, 19, 20, 26
Treviño, Victor, 118
La Tribuna, 37
Tropical, 64
Truman, Harry, 38*f*

undocumented workers. *See* immigrant conflicts
unemployment, Depression years, 39–40
United Farm Workers Association (UFWA), 83, 97
United Nations, 122
University of Houston, 82, 89–90, 111, 122, 128
Urteaga, Frank, 62*f*

Valdez, Ruth, 78
Valenzuela, Dianna, 135*f*
Valenzuela, Jesús, 135*f*
Valley Serenaders, 64
Vara, Richard C., 101
Vara, Rudy, 58, 118
Varela, Al, 102
Vázquez, Alfonso, 78, 79*f*, 83*f*, 85*f*
Vásquez, Andy, 90
Vásquez, Gabriel, 129, 132
Vásquez, Hilda, 62*f*
Vásquez, Kris, 88
Vásquez, Margarito "Gunny," 137*f*
Vega, Rodolfo Avila de la, 37
Vega, Victor, 100
Velásquez, Alfonso, 76*f*
Velásquez, Consuelo, 62*f*
Velázquez, Johnny, 64

Venzor, Luis, 27
Vera, Juanita, 85
Vermeersch, Benitia, 24–25
Vietnam War, 90–91, 101
Villagómez, Delfina, 24*f*
Villagómez, Ramón, 24*f*, 89
Villanueva, Rita, 104
Villareal, Ernest, 58
Viva Humphrey-Muskie Clubs, 85
Viva Johnson-Humphrey Clubs, 85
Viva Kennedy-Johnson Clubs, 79
La Voz, 117

War for Independence, Texas, 10–11, 12–13
Welch, Louie (and administration), 84, 87, 88
Wesley Community Center, 113
Wesley Community House, 43, 87, 99
White, Theodore H., 81
Whitmire, John, 131
Whitmire, Kathy (and administration), 116–117, 121, 122*f*
Williams, Loretta Ramírez, 137*f*
women's organizations/leaders: during the 1930s, 48, 49–50*f*; during the 1940s, 61; during the 1950s, 62*f*, 68*f*, 69; during the 1970s, 97–98; during the 1980s, 119–124; during the 1990s, 128, 131–133, 134–136
Woodmen of the World (WOW), 18
Works Progress Administration (WPA), 44–45, 46*f*
World War II, 52–55
Wortham Theater Center, 112*f*
WPA (Works Progress Administration), 44–45

Yañez, Lorenzo, 37
Yarborough, Ralph, 72
Young Women's Christian Association (YWCA), 48, 61, 98